SEPTIMA CLARK AND
THE CIVIL RIGHTS MOVEMENT

READY FROM WITHIN

Edited with an Introduction by

Cynthia Stokes Brown

Africa World Press, Inc.

P. O. Box 1892
Trenton, New Jersey 08607

P. O. Box 48
Asmara, ERITREA

Africa World Press, Inc.

P. O. Box 1892 P. O. Box 48
Trenton, New Jersey 08607 Asmara, ERITREA

First Printing AWP Edition 1990
Second Printing, September 1991
Third Printing, March 1996

Cover Design by Ife Nii Owoo

Library of Congress Catalog Card Number: 90-80668

ISBN: 0-86543-173-6 Cloth
       0-86543-174-4 Paper

About the Editor

CYNTHIA STOKES BROWN serves as Associate Professor of Education at Dominican College in San Rafael, California. She also co-directs Global Education Marin, a consortium that promotes global education in the secondary and elementary schools of Marin County. Her earlier writing includes *Literacy in Thirty Hours: Paulo Freire's Process in Northeast Brasil* (1975) and *Alexander Meiklejohn: Teacher of Freedom* (1981).

Cynthia Stokes Brown spent the first twenty-four years of her life in the South—growing up in western Kentucky and getting educated at Duke University and at Johns Hopkins University. In Baltimore she taught high school for two years and received a Ph.D. in the history of education from Johns Hopkins. After a year in Cleveland, she escaped the confines of Anglo-Saxon culture by living for two years in northeast Brazil as the wife of a Peace Corps physician. She now makes her home in Berkeley, California, and is the mother of two sons.

IVOR BROWN

Acknowledgments

AT ITS HEART, this book is a collaboration. Together Septima Clark and I re-created her story, something that neither of us could have achieved working alone.

I want to thank the many others who joined our collaboration. Herbert R. Kohl brought us together. When he first met Septima at Highlander Center in May 1979, Herb realized the possibilities of our working together and arranged for us to meet. Herb also introduced me to Myles Horton when he came to the Bay Area fundraising for Highlander Center. Myles sat in my kitchen and told me stories until I understood. Judy Kohl, together with Herb and Myles, read the many versions of the manuscript and helped me figure out what to do next. Without these three, there would be no book.

Thanks to Eliot Wigginton for his fine interviews with Bernice Robinson, Dorothy Cotton, and Andrew Young; to Sue Thrasher for helping me locate these interviews and all the other treasures in the Highlander Center archives; to Rosa Parks, Virginia Durr, and Bernice Robinson for filling me in.

For valuable suggestions and encouragement, I am indebted to Glenn Myles, Peggy Reimann, Lucy Massey Phenix, Daphne Muse, Jean Wiley, Thom Hiers, Toby Sherry, Colin Greer, Sydney Clemens, Jack Robbins, Sophie Heltai, the late Bradford Chambers, Rita Davies and her class in Mendocino, and my students—especially Gail Thomas, Mike Fanning, and Jancie Hughes.

My parents, Bud and Louise Stokes, and my friends since childhood—Mary Lu Mitchell, Horace Cox, and Stina and F.O. Baker, helped me put my past together.

The San Francisco Foundation, through Bernice Brown, provided a grant to Dominican College that helped support my work.

Most of all, thanks to Jim, Erik, Ivor, and Jack, who were by my side.

At the end, of course, without the enthusiasm of Alice Walker, Robert Allen, and Belvie Rooks, the book would not have come to life. Many thanks to them and their production staff.

Contents

INTRODUCTION, by Cynthia Stokes Brown

Searching   3

Finding Septima Clark   6

Finding Rosa Parks   13

SEPTIMA'S STORY

PART I: THE MOVEMENT

Judge Waring   23

The Turning Point   30

Dismissal   35

Highlander and the First Citizenship School   41

Raid on Highlander   55

All Over the Deep South   60

Non-Violent Resistance   71

The Role of Women   77

PART II: THE BEGINNING AND THE END

Septima's Childhood   87

Teaching, Marriage, and Children   103

Retirement and Contentment   119

CHRONOLOGY   128

NOTE ON SOURCES   131

INTRODUCTION

by Cynthia Stokes Brown

Searching

IT IS DIFFICULT for young people to imagine what segregation was, now that it is legally gone in the United States. It is hard for newer generations to realize, whenever black and white people are gathered together at a high school commencement, or at a party, or in a restaurant, at a meeting, on a bus, or in a classroom, that only twenty-five years ago all over one large section of this country and in varying degrees in other sections, these gatherings could not have happened. They simply could not take place.

When I was a teenager in the fifties, the biggest fight I ever had with my father was not over when I could first wear a formal gown to go dancing. That was a minor fight. A major one, in my mind, was the time I arranged for my church group to visit the young people of a black church in my town.

My father refused to let me go. I stayed home, weeping in my room. My father knew the basic social fact in our town—that white people did not mix with black people. He believed that his friends and associates would not accept him if he permitted his daughter to do such a thing as visit a black church. He intended to live and be accepted in that town.

That town—Madisonville, in western Kentucky—consisted of about ten thousand people. A quarter of them were black and lived in separate areas on the edges of town. Since their areas had no pavement, it was simple even for a child to tell where they were. A few black people still lived in alleys behind white houses, but that pattern of blacks living behind whites was dying out.

An archway at the southern entrance to my town proclaimed it "The Best Town on Earth." From childhood on I had some serious doubts about whether that sign was telling the truth.

I thought that Madisonville had just about the craziest social system that anybody could possibly imagine. There was one whole set of facilities—schools, churches, stores, drinking fountains, funeral parlors—for black people, and another whole set for white people. Some places like buses, movie theaters or hospitals, the two groups could share as long as each group stayed in its own section. Other places, like parks, libraries, and swimming pools, were not available at all for black people.

I didn't know there was a word for that kind of system; no one ever mentioned "segregation" in my presence or wrote it in our newspapers. All I knew was that I was not supposed to relate to black people in the same way that I related to white people, and even that nobody told me directly.

The rules changed as I grew from infancy to school age, and no one explained the silent code to me. When I was three and four, I had a black "mother" who took care of me in the afternoons as I played. I could sit in her lap as long as I liked, while she sang to me and told stories.

A black woman, named Willie Mae Elliott, ran a bustling funeral parlor about six blocks from my house. My best white friend and I used to sit on the curb, waiting for Willie Mae to pick us up in her hearse on her way from the hospital to her funeral house, where we could play with our black friends.

But as soon as I attained the age of five, all my social contact with black people had to stop. They had to be treated in a different way than equals. My mother dismissed my black mother, for fear that she would bring disease—TB or polio—to us from her poor living quarters. No black children were present at the kindergarten I attended. I was suddenly cut off from a rich and happy association that I craved.

It felt to me as if I were in some kind of jail for white people. It kept me from being able to reach black people. It seemed that our jail, the one for whites, was set down inside the jail for blacks. They were outside our area, and they couldn't come inside to share our activities. Since the walls between the two prisons were invisible, I had to figure out where they were. It was not an easy thing to learn.

By the time I was a teenager I wanted to change it, to mix black and white people together and arrange society the way I thought it ought to be. I could never figure out how to do that, but as I was graduating from high school in the spring of 1956, the civil rights movement was beginning to get underway throughout the South. Within ten years segregation, as a legal system, would be overturned, and all of us would be set free from our jails of color.

But who set us free? Who figured out what steps to take to turn a whole social system on its head? How did they do it?

The end of the civil rights movement is often marked by the assassination of Martin Luther King, Jr., in 1968. In the years following that, my curiosity about the people who had put an end to segregation increased. I wanted to find out how they decided what to do first. I wanted to know if the actions they took had the consequences that they intended. I wondered if their fathers and mothers, or other relatives and friends, had tried to stand in their way.

I wanted to know who their leader was. I thought there had to be a single leader because newspapers and textbooks had given me the impression that there was always a single, famous man behind everything. Martin Luther King, Jr., seemed to be that man, but I wondered if he really had masterminded everything from the beginning.

I wanted to know who set up the system of segregation in the first place and why it had made sense to them. I wondered why black people had ever accepted it in the beginning and what eventually happened to the system that made it vulnerable to change.

This drive to understand how human affairs take place was so strong in me that I became a serious student of history. I majored in United States history in college and taught in high schools. But I never stopped wondering about the people who started the civil rights movement. Whoever they were, I wanted to meet them, to talk with them, to understand them.

5

Finding Septima Clark

I BEGAN TO ASK QUESTIONS of anyone who might know something about the civil rights movement. The person I met who knew most about it turned out to be a white man with a twinkle in his blue eyes named Myles Horton. Myles lived on a farm in the mountains of eastern Tennessee about six hundred miles from where I grew up in western Kentucky. I had never heard of Myles Horton while I was growing up, but I was able to get to know him years later when he visited Berkeley, California, where I live now.

Myles was always interested in the origins of things. He could tell me endless stories about the beginnings of the civil rights movement. He personally knew many of the people involved in it, including Mrs. Rosa Parks, the woman in Montgomery, Alabama, who wouldn't give up her seat in the back of the bus to a white man. That happened in December of 1955, the year I was a senior in high school. I vaguely remember reading about Mrs. Parks in the newspaper —something about how she was a cleaning lady who was just so tired after her day's work that she couldn't get up. Her feet hurt too much.

But Myles told me a different story. He told me how beautiful Mrs. Parks was, how dignified she was, how she worked as a seamstress in a big department store. He told me that she was the secretary of the Montgomery chapter of the National Association for the Advancement of Colored People, called the N, double A, C, P, and that she worked with the young people there. He also told me that she had been thinking for years about what could be done to overthrow segregation; she had watched its cruel effects on herself, her family, and her associates. Myles knew all this because the summer before she was arrested Mrs. Parks had spent two weeks at Myles' school in Tennessee.

This school was not like any other school I had ever heard about. It had no classes or bells or curriculum. Instead, it was a beautiful farm high in the mountains near Chattanooga where adults could come to talk and think. They could leave their communities where they faced serious problems and could get away to discuss them. Myles and his colleagues had built dormitories where people could stay; they had an extensive vegetable garden, a fine library, and instruments for making music. Those provided the framework of their school, which was called Highlander Folk School.

Another thing different about this school was that black people could go there and stay overnight along with white people. This couldn't happen anywhere else in the South during my childhood because all the southern states had laws against it. The laws said that black and white people couldn't marry each other, couldn't eat together, and couldn't stay overnight under the same roof. There had to be separate facilities for every function.

Myles chose not to obey those laws in Tennessee. He didn't believe they were just, and therefore he ignored them. As a teenager he had observed that ministers in his town would hold meetings where blacks and whites could talk, but then they would not eat lunch together. Myles resolved never to let that happen under his roof.

He started his school in 1932, during the Great Depression, and soon after that black people began going to it. Eventually it became known as the only place in the South where the races could "tea and pee" together.

Once Myles told me about a reporter who asked him how in the world he got black and white people to sit down and eat together. That was just unheard of in the South; many people believed it couldn't be done.

Myles told him it was really very simple. It took just three steps. First, you prepared the food. Second, you put it on the table. Third, you rang the bell.

7

Because he is thirty-four years older than I am, Myles was a wonderful source of information for me. He could help me understand things that happened when I was so young that I couldn't begin to figure them out.

For instance, he told me about the first big interracial meeting held in the South. It took place in Birmingham, Alabama, in 1938, the year I was born. Among the 1250 people who attended was Eleanor Roosevelt, the wife of President Franklin Roosevelt. The seating at the meeting was segregated according to local laws, but Mrs. Roosevelt insisted on sitting on the black side until the policemen asked her to move. That is how I began to understand why Mrs. Roosevelt was so hated by whites in my home town. I had never been able to figure that out, especially why the men in my town would hate the wife of the president of our country.

Eventually Myles told me about a black woman who first went to Highlander Folk School in the summer of 1954. Her name was Septima Clark, and she lived in Charleston, South Carolina. Already fifty-six years old when she first came to Highlander, she had been a teacher all her life. Not long after her first visit, she became Highlander's director of education.

Myles told me that Septima Clark could not be discouraged by anything. She decided that segregation could not be overturned until black people could vote. The way the law was written in many southern states, blacks had to be able to read parts of the state constitutions in order to register to vote. Mrs. Clark concluded that she would just have to get busy and teach black adults to read.

Someone else might have been discouraged by that task. In 1955 only about 25% of voting-age blacks were registered in the eleven deep south states. More than 3½ million weren't registered, and many of them couldn't read. Working with others, Mrs. Clark figured out how to teach them to read in two or three months time. And she didn't just teach them to read; she taught them how to stand up for their rights. She trained hundreds of other teachers to teach them, and by 1970 nearly 2 million more black people were voting than had been in 1955.

Myles Horton thought that Septima Clark had as much to do with getting the civil rights movement started as anybody else—and I had never heard of her. I had read many books about the Movement, but they never said one word about Septima Clark.

I wanted to find out why she was never mentioned. Was it because she was a woman? But then, Myles Horton was almost never mentioned either, and he was a man.

Maybe it was because Horton and Clark worked in ways that historians and reporters don't usually find out about. Maybe they really didn't know about Clark's work. But maybe they did, and chose not to tell about it.

I had to find out more. Although no one else had written a book about Septima Clark, I discovered that she had written one herself, called *Echo in My Soul*. I pored through it, but it stopped exactly where her most exciting work started— when she was sixty years old and the civil rights movement was finally going in earnest. If I wanted to find out how Mrs. Clark worked during the Movement days, my only recourse was to go to Charleston and ask her myself.

I arrived in August, 1979, feeling nervous and excited. I could stay only six days, and I had much to learn. I didn't know anything about Charleston—about what kind of a place it was or how it got that way.

Also, I was not sure what kind of a person Septima Clark was. Maybe she wouldn't like me. What if we just didn't click? After all, why should we? It seemed we were as different as people could be. She was an elderly black woman, eighty-one years old, who had lived most of her life in South Carolina. I was forty years younger, a white woman who had left the South in early adulthood to live in Baltimore, Maryland; in Cleveland, Ohio; in Recife and Fortaleza, Brazil; and finally in Berkeley, California. Would we have anything in common?

I had already decided that I wanted to write a book about

Mrs. Clark. But to write such a book I had to learn many secrets from her, secrets about the ways in which she had resisted the cruelty of white people. Why should she be willing to tell those secrets to someone she had just met, especially if that someone were white?

Charleston is a spectacular city. It lies on a peninsula between two huge rivers draining water from the coastal hills down to the Atlantic Ocean. Its harbor is protected by islands seven miles offshore—the famous sea-islands of the southern Atlantic coast. They give Charleston a cozy, secure, nestled feeling that is very different from the rugged pounding of the Pacific Ocean familiar to me.

A friend whisked me off in his VW van to his home on Sullivan's Island, which lies off the coast slightly to the north of Charleston, across the Cooper River. On Sullivan's Island stand the remains of Fort Sumter, where Confederate soldiers fired the first shots of the Civil War at Yankee soldiers who were trying to replenish their supplies. As we passed Fort Sumter, with my friend talking in the soft tones of Charlestonese, with the temperature and the humidity both hovering around 95, I felt myself sinking rapidly into the Old South.

It was late in the afternoon on that Saturday when I telephoned Mrs. Clark's house. She was expecting me. I had written, and she had consented to a week of interviews. "Please come right over," she said, eager to begin.

A fifteen-minute drive over the Cooper River, through the middle of Charleston's peninsula, took me to Mrs. Clark's white frame house on President Street. Across the front of the house stretched a screened-in porch, comfortably outfitted with a hanging swing and pots of plants.

Mrs. Clark took me right in and introduced me to the people she lived with. First, there were two enormously tall grandsons in their early twenties. They were living with their grandmother while they worked as life-guards during the summer. Another grandson, David, age ten, had spent most of the summer with her, but he had left just a few days before. Mrs. Clark referred to her grandchildren as her "grands," an expression I had never heard before.

Upstairs lived Mrs. Clark's sister, Lorene. She spent most of her time in bed, for she suffered from Parkinson's disease. She was as tiny, frail, and timid as Mrs. Clark was sturdy, bustling, and outgoing.

It was difficult to convince myself that Mrs. Clark was eighty-one years old. Her right eye drooped a bit, but no other physical trait suggested her years. A proper greying wig covered her own hair, hiding whatever it might tell. Her smooth chocolate skin said nothing about age, the way white people's skin does. Relaxed and comfortable in a housedress and slippers, Mrs. Clark showed me a cabinet filled with plaques and awards before she settled down on the sofa. Together we paged through her album of family photos, citations, and Christmas messages. Over us, peering out of imposing portraits, watched her father, gently tolerant, and her mother, fiercely proud.

Mrs. Clark was enjoying herself immensely, sharing once again all the familiar relics of her years. But I was growing more and more confused and agitated. How were we ever going to cover everything? How could I make sense of it? I had come armed with a six-page list of questions, and I hadn't even asked one yet.

Filled with anxiety, I returned to Sullivan's Island to sleep. I should have been relieved, for my worst fear had been allayed. Mrs. Clark certainly didn't have any trouble relating to a white person. I found her completely at ease about sharing her life with me. But I was overwhelmed by her accounts; there seemed no way that I could absorb so much in so short a time.

Mrs. Clark's agenda for Sunday morning consisted of attending Bethel Methodist Church where her family had belonged for some eighty years. She invited me to join her, and we sat in the pew named for her mother, Victoria Anderson Poinsette. At last the sweet feeling of ease filled me. I, too, had grown up attending a Methodist church, and all the words and songs were my own—the rituals of my childhood and adolescence. The preacher introduced me; the congregation welcomed me; I felt at home where I belonged.

Back at Mrs. Clark's home, she effortlessly asembled a feast of yams, chicken, rice, and okra. After everyone was fed, as we lingered over our food, she began to tell me stories of the dangers she had faced. My tape recorder was stored in the other room, but I didn't mind. We were setting the pattern for our work together. Everyday we would discuss another segment of her life and work, and then we would record it on tape. She would tell her narrative, while I listened attentively, asking questions or reminding her of details she had told me earlier. After a week I had the story of her life on tape.

Or so I thought. After I returned to Berkeley and transcribed her tape, I saw once more how little I understood about the context of Mrs. Clark's life. There were many gaps that I couldn't fill; I didn't know enough about the other people in the drama. I would have to learn a great deal more before I could put her story together in a way that would make sense to me.

Finding Rosa Parks

IN MY READING I occasionally came across the name of E.D. Nixon. Several people had told me that E.D. Nixon was the real organizer behind the bus boycott in Montgomery. They had told me that he was a working-class person, not usually trusted by middle-class people, that he was an active member of the Brotherhood of Sleeping Car Porters, and that he served as the president of the NAACP in Montgomery. When I read the following anecdote told by E.D. Nixon, I wanted to know much more about him and about the woman he described, Mrs. Rosa Parks:

> I haven't seen anybody yet that wanted to believe any-
> thing about the Movement except something what the
> Reverend King said. I ain't seen nobody yet. . . . If you
> gonna say somethin' that Rev. King didn't do, you're
> almost spittin' in folks' face. I was on an airplane coming
> down from New York some time ago, sittin beside a
> lady, and she asked me who I was and I told her. She
> said, "Oh, you're down in Montgomery, Alabama."
> She said, "Lord, I don't know what'ud happened to the
> black people if Rev. King hadn't went to town."
> I said, "If Mrs. Parks had got up and given that
> white man her seat, you'd never aheard of Rev. King."
> When I said that, man, I as well as spit in her face.

By reading and talking to people I learned the basic outline of what happened in Montgomery, Alabama, starting on the first of December, 1955. On that Thursday Mrs. Parks was sitting in the back of the bus in the section where black people were supposed to be. Her seat was in the front row of the black section. When the front of the bus filled up, the bus driver told her and two others to give their seats to white people. The other two did, but Mrs. Parks refused to stand up. The driver stopped and called the police; they arrested Mrs. Parks and took her to jail. From there she called E.D. Nixon, who came, paid her bail, and released her from jail.

The police charged Mrs. Parks with breaking the Alabama law that required segregated seating on buses and required blacks to give up their seats to whites as the bus filled. They could have charged her with disobeying an officer or with creating a public disturbance. That is what they usually did. But this time they charged her in a way that invited a challenge to the law itself.

E.D. Nixon, from his experience as president of the NAACP, realized that this was the case he had been waiting for. Other similar cases had come up before, but either the charge was wrong or the person was wrong. This case was right. The black people of Montgomery would support Mrs. Parks because she was known to them as the secretary of the NAACP. She had an inner calm and dignity that meant she could hold up under interrogation in court. Nixon and his colleagues saw that this might be the case that would go all the way to the U.S. Supreme Court.

However, the charges against Mrs. Parks could probably have been dismissed on a technicality. She could have chosen not to undergo months of trials, publicity, and anxiety. But she decided to press her case to the U.S. Supreme Court, if necessary, whatever that might mean to her personally.

Nixon organized a mass meeting to discuss the arrest of Mrs. Parks; for the place he chose the downtown church of Martin Luther King, Jr., a twenty-six-year-old Baptist minister who had just moved to town the previous year. At the meeting it was decided that black people would boycott the buses in Montgomery until their demands were met.

For one year the boycott continued. People walked, or carpooled, or were picked up by their white employers. Since black people constituted about seventy-five percent of the bus company's patrons, it lost a great deal of money. The desperate company raised its fares from 10¢ to 15¢ for adults and from 5¢ to 8¢ for students. Rev. King began to preach about non-violence as the way to secure social change.

Mrs. Parks' case did reach the U.S. Supreme Court. It ruled in November, 1956, that Alabama's bus law was unconstitutional. In December black people in Montgomery got back on buses in which they no longer had to sit in the back. Three months later, in order to spread the idea of non-violent resistance to injustice, black ministers organized the first southern-wide black civil rights organization. They called it the Southern Christian Leadership Conference, or SCLC for short.

But Rosa Parks' personal life had a harsher outcome. Soon after the bus boycott began, Montgomery Fair Department Store, where Mrs. Parks worked, re-organized its departments so that it no longer needed her. It laid her off. Nobody in Montgomery was willing to hire her. Since her husband was ill, she was the sole support of him and her mother. Without work for Rosa, the Parks family was eventually forced to leave Montgomery. In December, 1957, they boarded a train for Detroit, where Mrs. Parks had a brother working for Ford Motor Company.

Those were the bare facts, but they didn't satisfy me. I wanted to know what was in Mrs. Parks' mind when she refused to give up her seat. Had she been planning for months to do that? Did her husband want her to do it? Did her mother? How did the idea come to her?

Actually getting to meet Mrs. Parks seemed too much for me to hope for, but it did come about. In December, 1979, a group of people in Berkeley, called the East Bay Friends of Highlander, decided to honor both Rosa Parks and Septima Clark at a testimonial dinner. That is when I learned that Mrs. Parks was still living in Detroit, where she was working as a receptionist to U.S. Representative John Conyers. Mrs. Clark and Mrs. Parks agreed to come to Berkeley, partly because they hadn't seen each other for many years and wanted to be re-united. They also wanted to help raise money for

Highlander Center, where they had met each other. On May 1, 1980, three hundred people in the Bay Area spent an evening together, honoring two mothers of the civil rights movement and understanding it better.

Mrs. Parks astonished me; she was not at all who I expected her to be. She was no flamboyant, confident, assertive heroine. On the contrary, she was a petite, quiet, timid woman who avoided the limelight whenever possible—just the sort of person I had always thought one would have to stop being if one were ever to have any effect on the world at all.

My next surprise occurred in the restroom, where I accompanied Mrs. Parks when she wanted to straighten up before the ordeal of meeting with reporters and photographers. She removed her white, crocheted cloche, pulled out a few hairpins, and her braids fell below her waist in a cascade of thick, wavy hair that Rapunzel would have envied.

When Mrs. Parks saw the astonishment on my face, she chuckled softly, "Well, many of my ancestors were Indians. I never cut my hair because my husband liked it this way. It's a lot of trouble, and he's been dead a number of years, but I still can't bring myself to cut it."

Gradually it was dawning on me that people of different races in this country had gotten together long before the civil rights movement. Racial purity, I saw, was a fiction of the southern legislators who had passed laws to make interracial love a crime. They called it miscegenation, and hoped to spread the idea that only the most outrageous outlaws would participate in such a thing. Yet here before me stood the heroine of the black struggle for civil rights—and she herself was partly native American. No one had ever mentioned that.

At the dinner Mrs. Parks spoke directly about what Mrs. Clark had meant to her.

> I am always very respectful and very much in awe of the presence of Septima Clark because her life story makes the effort that I have made very minute. I only hope that there is a possible chance that some of her

great courage and dignity and wisdom has rubbed off on me. When I first met her in 1955 at Highlander, when I saw how well she could organize and hold things together in this very informal setting of interracial living, I had to admire this great woman. She just moved through the different workshops and groups as though it was just what she was made to do, in spite of the fact that she had to face so much opposition in her home state and lost her job and all of that. She seemed to be just a beautiful person, and it didn't seem to shake her.

While on the other hand, I was just the opposite. I was tense, and I was nervous, and I was upset most of the time. I can't describe my attitude too well, not in this polite company. However, I was willing to face whatever came, not because I felt that I was going to be benefitted or helped personally, because I felt that I had been destroyed too long ago. But I had the hope that the young people would be benefitted by equal education, should the Supreme Court decision of 1954 be carried out as it should have been.

Mrs. Parks went on to describe what Highlander and Myles Horton had meant to her.

Myles Horton just washed away and melted a lot of my hostility and prejudice and feeling of bitterness toward white people, because he had such a wonderful sense of humor. I often thought about many of the things he said and how he could strip the white segregationists of their hardcore attitudes and how he could confuse them, and I found myself laughing when I hadn't been able to laugh in a long time.

I actually did not think in terms of non-violence and Christian love in connection with the Movement (we didn't call it the Movement—we just called it survival) until Dr. Martin Luther King came to Montgomery, and I heard him speak. But it was a long time before I could feel the philosophy he was teaching, just as it was a while before I could realize where Myles Horton was coming from and what his dedication meant. I had a hard lesson to learn, that I could not help others free their hearts and minds of racial prejudice unless I would do all that I could within myself to straighten out my own thinking and to feel and respond to kindness, to goodwill from wherever it came, whether it was the southerner, northerner, or any race. So I am very pleased to be with this wonderful group of people, this great fellowship of human beings, and to know that you feel that I have made the type of contribution that merits this honor.

Myles Horton, Cynthia Brown, and Septima Clark at the Coastal Ridge Research and Education Center, Point Arena, California, in May, 1980.

As Mrs. Parks talked, the story of the civil rights move-ment began to fall into place for me. Mrs. Parks had been able to do what she did because of Myles Horton and Septima Clark and E.D. Nixon. Events had not happened in a random way; they were hooked together through the relationships that people had established with each other. There had been no single leader.

By means of the testimonial dinner I met many more people who had been part of starting the civil rights move-ment. Through them I found others and finally, in the summer of 1986, seven years after I met Septima Clark, I was ready to finish her story.

Mrs. Clark's story may not be easy for us today to understand. She lived in a fully segregated society that has now largely disappeared. She refers to many people and events that are no longer familiar. To imagine ourselves in her shoes takes a great deal of effort.

Not only is the past unfamiliar to us, but Mrs. Clark's view of it has changed. She told me this story when she was eighty-one years old, from how she remembered and inter-preted her life in 1979. If she had told me her story twenty years earlier, when she was sixty-one, it would have been quite unlike this version.

The main difference is that this story is told from a feminist perspective. After the civil rights movement Mrs. Clark took part in the women's liberation movement and learned to comprehend her own story, as well as that of women in general, in a framework very different from that through which she experienced her life as it happened. When men who knew her in the 1960s read this story, they say, "But that's not how she felt back then." No, it's not, but it is how she felt at the age of eighty-one.

This version of Septima Clark's story is not only hers. It is also mine, because I have shaped it in several ways. I have decided the order in which to tell it. I have shortened it by choosing what to include out of the much longer account that Mrs. Clark told me. At the same time I have lengthened it by paraphrasing some of her comments and by adding connective lines that add background, accuracy, and reflection to her story. Recorded here is Mrs. Clark's account given at the age of eighty-one, as interpreted by me at the age of forty-eight.

I have carefully preserved Mrs. Clark's words and diction to keep them as close as possible to exactly what she said as she talked to me. But Mrs. Clark can talk in many different ways, depending on who her audience is, or who she imagines her audience to be. She speaks many varieties of the English language—from a very African version as it used to be spoken on Johns Island, through black Charlestonese, white Charlestonese, white Appalachian English, to standard university English. With me, she often relaxed into a comfortable sort of down-home southern English that we share. But at other times, as she imagined a book audience, she formulated her story into a more nearly standard, middle-class English. I treasure these changes of diction; they reveal the cultural skills of a woman who learned to be at home with many races and classes of people.

Cynthia Stokes Brown
June, 1986
Berkeley, California

SEPTIMA'S STORY

PART I: THE CIVIL RIGHTS MOVEMENT

Judge Waring

MY NAME IS SEPTIMA POINSETTE CLARK. I was born at 105 Wentworth Street in Charleston, South Carolina, on May 3, 1898. When I was seven, my parents moved to Henrietta Street. 26 Henrietta Street. After I grew up, I moved to different places in South Carolina to teach, but I always had the home I bought here in Charleston. This German that my brother was working with had that house for sale. It wasn't but two thousand and five hundred dollars. I was able to get it in 1927 with my little bit of money and get it all paid for. So we had our own house at 17 Henrietta Street, the street I had grown up on.

I moved back to Charleston in 1947, and that is the part of my story I want to tell about first. Later on I will go back and tell about my growing up and the early years of my teaching.

I want to start my story with the end of World War II because that is when the civil rights movement really got going, both for me personally and for people all over the South. After World War II the men were coming home from fighting in Europe and Africa, and they weren't going to take segregation any more.

In 1947 I got a job in Charleston teaching seventh grade at the newest school in the system, the Henry P. Archer School. But soon my assignment was changed, and I was put in charge of a group of problem pupils in grades four through seven. Each period these children would come to me from their home rooms, and we did what was actually remedial reading. It was challenging work, and we made considerable progress.

23

I hadn't been in Charleston long before I got involved in civic activities. Among other organizations I had a special interest in the work of the Young Women's Christian Association. There was a dual system in Charleston, with separate white and black "Y's." Soon after I returned to Charleston I became chairman of the black "Y's" committee on administration. My courage was soon to be tested. It came about this way.

At the time the judge of the United States Court for the eastern disrict of South Carolina was a Charlestonian named Julius Waties Waring. He was the same judge who had decreed that the salaries of school teachers in South Carolina, black and white, had to be equalized. I knew him principally because of that decision; since he was Charleston born and bred, I saw his name in the newspapers frequently.

I knew that Judge Waring had grown up in the upper-class area of Charleston and had married an aristocratic girl. He was a personal friend of both the U.S. senators from South Carolina, one of whom just spouted racist rhetoric. When Waring was appointed U.S. judge, he was considered a person who would protect the southern way of life.

But Judge Waring transformed himself as he sat in his judge's chair. I heard him say once: "You know, a judge has to live with his conscience. I would sit in the courtroom, and I would see black men coming in that I knew were decent men, and they were considered bums and trash because they were black. And I would see white men that I knew were bums, and they were considered gentlemen. I just couldn't take it any longer."

When I returned to Charleston, black people still could not vote in the Democratic primary elections. There weren't many blacks who were registered voters, but those who were registered Democrats could not vote in the primary election, where you elect the candidates your party will run in the final election.

That rule to keep blacks out of primary elections was made way back in 1896, just before I was born. The legislature passed that law as part of setting up segregation in South

Carolina. The U.S. Supreme Court finally ruled against white primaries in 1944, but southern states were still following their own rules.

A number of black people had gotten to the place where their children were going north to college, and they were coming back talking about the injustices we had in Charleston where we could not vote in the Democratic primary. It had gotten to the place where the younger generation felt very bad about it.

After Judge Waring realized how wrong it was to keep blacks out of the primary, he decided to change it. In 1947 he ruled that blacks must be permitted to vote in the next primary, and he told the leaders of the Democratic Party that the court would hold them personally responsible for carrying out this ruling.

Several days before the election some of the whites made a statement that if blacks attempted to vote in the primary, then blood would be running down the streets like water. Judge Waring said to them, and had the press print it, that "If that happens, I'll put you in jail, and you'll stay there for the rest of your life. These people have a right to vote, and so they will vote."

You know, that was a quiet election. Election day used to be a terrible thing around Charleston. Guns were always out. During the election just before this one a young white reporter was killed. There would always be some death. But Judge Waring stopped that.

Just reading about Judge Waring I became really enthused about him. I thought, "This is a wonderful man to come forth and say that blacks should vote." At the YWCA we were going to have a special day, and I thought, "Now, if Judge Waring could say that, his wife might be able to say something to Negro women." In 1945 Judge Waring had divorced his first wife and had married Elizabeth Avery, a native of Detroit.

Another lady from the "Y" and I went to Mrs. Waring's house at 9 o'clock one night to ask her to speak. She was very glad to do it. But somehow or other the newspaper got hold of it, and all hell broke forth. Evidently somebody saw us going into that house, and they decided that this could not be.

I started getting obscene phone calls. I'd pick up the telephone, and they'd say: "Who in the hell do you think you are? You are a damn fool to ask Judge Waring's wife to speak." I'd say, "Thank you," and put down the phone.

Right away I decided that I'd better go and tell Mrs. Waring that if black people would ask her not to speak, would she let me know, but if white people would ask her not to speak, would she decide that she was going to speak regardless.

I went down to the Warings' house again. Judge Waring told me, "Now, Septima, the thing to do is to put somebody at each one of the places where you turn the lights on. You're going to have to have a man standing there, because if the Klan comes in, the first thing they're going to do is turn your lights out, and then you'll have a terrible time."

That's what I did. I got men to stand by all the lights in the hall of the YWCA. But no Klan came, only two or three white women. Mrs. Waring called the white people in Charleston decadent and low-down. I think she did it because they were mean. The reporters were there, and Mrs. Waring passed out a copy of her speech, saying, "Take this speech and put it in the paper just as it is. Don't change a word."

They printed that speech word for word. For three days after that meeting the town talked about Mrs. Waring and what she had said.

After that, the Warings were terribly harassed and persecuted. Their friends abandoned them. Not one white person would have dinner with them, or even drink tea with them. The white hairdressers refused to wash Mrs. Waring's hair. And when Judge Waring went to get his hair cut, a guard had to go with him and sit until he got his hair cut. They had to guard him day and night.

The Warings reached out to their black friends. Of course, a lot of blacks wouldn't go to the Warings' house. The Warings invited them to tea one night, and they wouldn't go. A few of us went to dinner. I had to say to myself that if these people invite me, surely I should go. Why should I be one who says not to go? All of these things you had to make up in your mind to do because too many of the blacks were against your going to the Warings' anyway. I had to make a decision to go regardless of what happened.

When I went to Judge Waring's home to dinner I, too, felt real worried. I always had to have my hair straightened, and I tried to have a new dress. Mrs. Waring told me that wasn't necessary. I was glad she could tell me that, but I thought it had to be.

At the Warings' I met many of the mulatto people of Charleston, and I wasn't considered too well by that group because they were very fair-skinned people with straight hair. My mother was a washerwoman, and my father had been a slave, so I wasn't considered one of them. But because of the way I could talk about the things I knew about, the injustices, they listened. By that time I had been to several universities, and I had studied a good bit about history, the history of government, and economics. These things had made an impression on me. I don't know whether they ever learned to like me too well, but they listened to me.

I was very happy for the kinds of people that I could meet at Mrs. Waring's house. I couldn't meet them otherwise. They would not have come to my house. I wasn't good enough. Neither could I go to their house. I couldn't even play cards or bridge with them, not at all. But this was the kind of caste and class thing that we had in Charleston.

I had a feeling that if I could eat at Judge Waring's house, at any white person's house, then they should be able to drink a cup of tea or do something at my house. So I invited Judge and Mrs. Waring and two others to have tea with me one afternoon, and they did come. My mother was sick in bed at the time, and I had taken her meal to her bedside. But she couldn't eat; she was too worried about it. My neighbors on my street were also worried. They said, "As long as Septima Clark have them white people coming to her house, we're gonna always have trouble."

Then my principal got worried about it, too. He saw

me coming out of Mrs. Waring's house from dinner one Sunday, and he said, "That's a dangerous thing to do. How in the world could you do it?"

At a faculty meeting at my school, they all told me how wrong they thought it was for me to go to the Warings' house. They said it just proved what white people were saying, that the real reason that blacks wanted integration was to socialize with whites.

I waited until they finished. Then I asked the principal if I could ask him a question.

"I would like to ask you if anyone decided for you whom you would marry."

"No, of course not," he replied. "I decided for myself."

Then I asked one of the women teachers, "Did anyone tell you what kind of car to buy and how much to pay for it?"

"No," she said. "I did that myself. It's my car. Why shouldn't I have made those decisions?"

Then I turned to a teacher who put a big emphasis on clothes; she was probably our best-dressed teacher.

"Did anybody tell you what type of dresses to buy and what stores to buy them at?" I asked

"Of course not," she replied, a bit indignantly.

"Well, I can see that you all make decisions for yourselves," I told them. "The principal decided what woman he wished to marry, and I think that no one should tell a man or woman who to marry. And you—" I pointed to the first woman I had questioned, "selected the car you bought, and I'm sure you had a perfect right to do that, just as you—" I pointed to the woman who loved to dress beautifully, "have every right to select your own clothes. In the same way," I looked them in the eyes, "I think that I have a right to select my own friends. I feel that nobody has a right to tell me who my friends must be any more than I have a right to tell the principal who his wife will be, or you what kind of car to buy, or you what sort of clothes you should wear."

The meeting closed, but I knew they were quite angry with me. After that there were many times, I'm sure, when it was hard for them to say a pleasant word to me or about me, all because of my association with the Warings.

The Warings did not get to finish out their years here in Charleston. They moved to New York City in 1950. They did that because when Mrs. Waring was sitting on a couch in their living room, someone threw a block of cement through the window. It nearly hit her, but it didn't. Then when she went to get some letters mimeographed, the woman refused and said, "Please don't come in here, because if you do you're going to ruin my business, and I won't be able to stay here any longer." Judge Waring used to go and hold court in the upper part of New York and in California, down at San Diego. When those courts were cancelled, he decided that they had better get out of here, which they did.

They lived in New York City until they died in 1968. He was buried in January, and she died in November. He had two hundred blacks and twelve whites at his funeral, and she had nine of us at hers. She said she didn't want none of the hypocrites at her funeral, and she didn't have any. They were both buried in Charleston, right up in Magnolia Cemetery overlooking the harbor.

They had one laugh from the grave, though. They gave his retirement money to the College of Charleston, and it has to be used for a black student to live on campus. Of course, at that time the College of Charleston did not allow black people to go there. It took the college until 1976 to spend that money. Now black students can live on the campus. That has come out of Judge Waring's will.

The Turning Point

IN 1952 THERE WAS a childhood education meeting in Washington D.C., and a worker from the black "Y" in Charleston, a Mrs. Anna Kelly, went to that meeting. There were some things that she wanted to discuss with both blacks and whites, and she couldn't discuss them down here because we couldn't have a black and white meeting together. Teachers couldn't meet together, and neither could community people. They had to meet separately.

At that meeting Mrs. Kelly asked where in the South blacks and whites could meet together and talk over the problems that they talked about in that workshop. People told her that there was only one place—at the Highlander Folk School near Chattanooga.

Mrs. Kelly decided to go there in the summer of '53, and she asked me would I sit on the desk of the YWCA while she was away. When she came back, she said, "Oh, that's a wonderful place. You don't even have to spend a nickel. You go up there, and they feed you, and they sleep you, and they ride you, and so everything is wonderful."

I decided I should go to a place like that, so the next summer I went up, and I found what she said was true. I even found that blacks and whites were sleeping in the same room—that surprised me.

That's when I met Myles Horton and his wife Zilphia. Myles used to open the workshops by asking the people what they wanted to know, and he would close it with, "What you going to do back home?"

Zilphia played an accordian, and she would always lead

the singing. She was a very good singer, and she had the songs of the people of the mountains, of the low country, of the labor unions, and whatever group. When she died, we really missed her.

Myles and Zilphia came to Charleston when we were having a testimonial for Judge Waring. Judge Waring had become the most hated fellow below Broad Street in Charleston; the white people learned to dislike him greatly. They said they disliked him because he married a Yankee woman. To marry a Yankee in their face was terrible. He also was hated because he had opened the Democratic primary to black people. For that, the black people of Charleston gave him a testimonial. That night we had large numbers of people at a school we were able to get. Afterwards Zilphia stayed at my house, and Mrs. Waring stayed at one of the other black women's house.

I kept up my contacts with Myles and Zilphia and the Highlander Folk School. While I was at Highlander for the first time, the Supreme Court decided that segregation shall be no more. We were really happy over that, and I felt wonderful. But I didn't yet have the feeling that this thing was really a part of me.

I went to Highlander twice the first summer in '54, and the following summer I used my car to transport three groups of six persons each to Highlander workshops. At the end of that summer we held a workshop to develop leadership, which I was directing. That was when I met Rosa Parks.

At that time Mrs. Parks lived in Montgomery, Alabama. Her husband was a barber, and he used to shave and cut hair for all of the high-class whites. Rosa was working with the youth group of the National Association for the Advancement of Colored People, or the N, double A, C, P, for short.

Rosa got to Highlander because she knew Virginia Durr, a great friend of Myles Horton, the director of Highlander. Rosa and Virginia got to know each other by Rosa being a seamstress and Virginia's husband being the only lawyer in Montgomery who would take the legal cases brought by the

NAACP. Working with the NAACP, Rosa was under fire. Virginia stayed under fire because she was a white woman who dared to take sides with blacks.

First Virginia Durr wrote a letter and asked that we send money for Rosa to come up to Highlander, which we did. Then Virginia took Rosa to Atlanta and saw her on a bus to Highlander.

We had a large group of people at that workshop. It was a two-week workshop on the United Nations. We knew that Rosa had been working with the youth group in Montgomery, so at the meeting I asked Rosa to tell how she was able to get the Freedom Train to come to Montgomery and get this youth group to go through the Freedom Train. She wouldn't talk at all at first.

People at the workshop knew only a little bit about the Freedom Train. It was being sent by the government around the country from Washington, D.C., as a lesson in democracy. It carried an exhibit of the original U.S. Constitution and the Declaration of Independence. Anyone could go inside for free, but segregation was not permitted.

One night up there in the bedroom (there were about six beds in one dormitory) everyone started singing and dancing, white kids and all, and they said, "Rosa, how in the world did you deal with that Freedom Train?"

Then she said, "It wasn't an easy task. We took our children down when the Freedom Train came, and the white and black children had to go in together. They wouldn't let them go in otherwise, and that was a real victory for us." But she said, "After that, I began getting obscene phone calls from people because I was president of the youth group. That's why Mrs. Durr wanted me to come up here and see what I could do with this same youth group when I went back home."

The next day in the workshop I say, "Rosa, tell these people how you got that Freedom Train to come to Montgomery." She hated to tell it. She thought that certainly somebody would go back and tell the white people. A teacher from Montgomery came at the same time, and she say she couldn't let them know she was coming to Highlander, because if these white people knew then she would have lost her job, too.

Anyway, Rosa got up and told that group about it. We, had somebody there from the United Nations, and they said to her, "If anything happens, you get in touch with me, and I'll be sure to see that you have your rights."

After the workshop, Rosa was afraid to go from Highlander to Atlanta. Myles sent me with her. She was afraid that somebody had already spoken, and she didn't know what was going to happen. I went with her to Atlanta and saw her in a bus going down to Montgomery. She felt much better then.

I guess she kept thinking about the things at the workshop. At the end of the workshops we always say, "What do you plan to do back home?" Rosa answered that question by saying that Montgomery was the cradle of the Confederacy, that nothing would happen there because blacks wouldn't stick together. But she promised to work with those kids,

Rosa Parks, Septima Clark, and Leona McCauley, mother of Rosa Parks, at Highlander Folk School in December, 1956.

and to tell them that they had the right to belong to the NAACP, that they had the right to do things like going through the Freedom Train. She decided that she was going to keep right on working with them.

Three months after Rosa got back to Montgomery, on December 1, 1955, she refused to get up from her seat on the bus. When I heard the news, I said, "Rosa? Rosa?" She was so shy when she came to Highlander, but she got enough courage to do that.

Rosa hadn't planned at Highlander that she was going to refuse to get up out of her seat. That evidently came to her that day after she got done at work. But many people at the Highlander workshop told about the discrimination on the buses. I guess practically every family around Montgomery had had trouble with people getting on buses. They'd had a hard time. They had a number of cases where bus drivers had beaten 15-year-olds who sat up to the front or refused to get up from their seat and give it to whites coming in. That was the kind of thing they had, and they had taken it long enough.

Now I had that all the time here in Charleston. I was living down on Henrietta Street. I caught the bus going to my school about a mile up. The Navy Yard men would be going to work at the same time. I would sit in that section that's designed for blacks. But if a white man came up, and the white section is all filled in, I'd have to stand up and give him my seat and stand up the rest of the way. I'd just get up and give him my seat. I knew I had to do it or be arrested. I'd sit in the back, but when that front got crowded they'd come to the back and you had to get up and give them your seat. That's what they call justice. I had to do that for a long time until Rosa refused, and then that changed.

I don't know why it was, but it seems like that did not make me angry. I always felt that there would be a time when I could work on things. I never felt that getting angry would do you any good other than hurt your own digestion—keep you from eating, which I liked to do.

Dismissal

BY THE TIME THAT ROSA PARKS refused to get up and give her seat to a white man, I had gotten into some trouble of my own back in Charleston. I began to realize that I might be dismissed from my position as an elementary teacher because I belonged to that same organization Rosa Parks did—the National Association for the Advancement of Colored People, the NAACP.

Let me go way back and tell you how I first heard about the NAACP. It started in 1909 in New York City, but I didn't hear of it until 1918. I was about twenty years old, and I was teaching on Johns Island, one of the islands off the coast of Charleston. That Presbyterian convention came to Johns Island, and I went down to the meeting. The man started talking about an organization that was to help people unjustly treated. It was just a dollar a year, so I joined while I was there on Johns Island.

Soon after that something happened that really led me to the NAACP. It was in the summer time, and I was working here in Charleston. We had a Jewish woman on King Street who had a watch in her apron pocket. We didn't have frigidaires then, and a boy was putting ice in her icebox. She thought he took her watch out of her apron pocket, and she had him arrested. The artist who was the head of the NAACP in Charleston found about it, and when we searched we found that her watch had gone to the laundry in her apron pocket and that boy was unjustly arrested. We got together, and we told her what big harm she had done to this boy. We said that somebody would call him jailbird and perhaps cause him to fight and that he had lost many weeks by spending that time in jail.

I felt real bad about that incident. I said, "Well, I must really get into that organization because we've got to see that things like this won't happen again." I became very fond of the NAACP, and from that time on I worked with it.

There weren't too many black people who considered the NAACP worthwhile. They were still afraid, you know, so it was a very small group at first. But after many years of work by its lawyers, the United States Supreme Court ruled, in 1954, that racial segregation in public schools was unconstitutional. After that decision, the school authorities in South Carolina passed out questionnaires to every teacher requiring us to list all the organizations we belonged to. I refused to overlook my membership in the NAACP, as some of the teachers did. I listed it.

The next year the South Carolina legislature passed a law that said that no city or state employee could belong to the NAACP. You see, our legislature was joining others across the deep South in a systematic campaign to wipe out the NAACP.

Our supervisor of Negro teachers was terribly concerned about it. She knew that she was going to lose her job because she was a member, and she did not want to give it up. She just got terribly ill in her mind. She became senile soon, and she died not too long after that, before they took her job away.

It wasn't too long before I got my letter of dismissal. The Board of Education wrote me that it would not be renewing my contract to teach remedial reading at the Henry Archer School. My goodness, somehow or other it really didn't bother me.

But it bothered my family. My sister said that when people called her she felt like she had something in her stomach, just like butterflies, working around. She was teaching then. I said, "You just let me answer the phone and tell the people I'm a member and I've been dismissed. I don't mind at all."

My mother had died by the time I was dismissed, but I know she would have said, "I told you so." She never joined the NAACP, nor my sister Edith. My brother Peter hasn't either. They weren't fighters. They didn't feel as if they could fight for freedom or for justice. They just didn't have that kind of feeling.

One hundred and sixty-nine teachers came from Washington and Baltimore to get our jobs, and there weren't but forty-two of us dismissed. Those teachers came down here because they had to have one year experience before they could teach in Baltimore or Washington. They came thinking they could get those jobs.

But they didn't get them. Other people already here got those jobs. Most of those forty-two teachers who were fired went to New York and Boston and other places in the North. A few of them came back and were able to get jobs teaching.

I never did try. I felt that they never would let me have one anyway because they considered me a Communist because I worked with the Highlander Folk School. I had been to Highlander two years before I was dismissed here. I know they felt that I was really a Communist then. I was too much of a head woman, a controversial leader, and I couldn't get any job here.

I feel the big failure in my life was trying to work with the black teachers to get them to realize, when that law was passed in South Carolina, that it was an unjust law. But there were such a few jobs that they didn't see how they could work against the law. I had the feeling that if all of them would say, "We are members of the NAACP," that the legislature would not have said, "All of you will lose your job," because that would mean thousands of children out on the streets at one time.

But I couldn't get them to see that. I signed my name to 726 letters to black teachers asking them to tell the state of South Carolina that it was unjust to rule that no city or state employee could belong to the NAACP. If whites could belong to the Ku Klux Klan, then surely blacks could belong to the NAACP.

I don't know why I felt that the black teachers would stand up for their rights. But they wouldn't. Most of them

Septima Clark at a testimonial party given in 1956 by her sorority, A.K.A., after she lost her job because of NAACP membership.

were afraid and became hostile. Only twenty-six of them answered my letter, and I wrote them that we should go and talk with the superintendent. Eleven decided that they would go to talk to the superintendent, but when it was time to go, there were only five of us. The superintendent did everything he could before he would see us. He was writing out some plans on a board. Finally he talked, and the only thing he did was to let us know that we were living far ahead of our time. That's what he said.

I considered that one of the failures of my life because I think that I tried to push them into something that they weren't ready for. From that day on I say, "I'm going to have to get the people trained. We're going to have to show them the dangers or the pitfalls that they are in, before they will accept." And it took many years.

You always have to get the people with you. You can't just force them into things. That taught me a good lesson, because when I went into Mississippi and Alabama I stayed behind the scene and tried to get the people in the town to push forward, and then I would come forth with ideas. But I wouldn't do it at first because I knew it was detrimental. That was a weakness of mine that I felt I had to strengthen. The people in the masses, though, do better than the teachers. They come out. They're willing to fight anyhow.

You know, I had to go away for twenty years from Charleston. I couldn't get a job here, nowhere in South Carolina. Not only that, but the black teachers here, my sorority, Alpha Kappa Alpha, gave me a testimonial. Alpha Kappa Alpha is an organization of black women college graduates. Do you know that at that party my sorors would not stand beside me and have their picture made with me? If they had, they would have lost their jobs.

I can't say that I kept from being frightened about this whole episode. For three solid months after I took a new job at Highlander Folk School I couldn't sleep. Night after night I stayed up listening to the tape of the workshop that we had conducted during the day. One morning, it must have been a September morning, I felt a kind of a free feeling in my mind, and I said, "Now I must have been right." I was able to fall asleep and to sleep after that. I decided that I had worried about the thing enough.

EDITOR'S NOTE:

The National Association for the Advancement of Colored People (NAACP) served as the dominant black protest movement for the first half of the twentieth century. Based in New York City, it was founded by highly educated white and black professionals. Initially all the top administrative positions were filled by whites, with one important exception; the Director of Publicity and Research was W.E.B. DuBois, the leading black intellectual of his time.

The NAACP used persuasion and legal action as its primary tactics. Even before the Brown decision in 1954, when the Supreme Court ruled against segregation in public schools, the NAACP had won important legal victories. For example, in 1915 the NAACP

*won a Supreme Court suit that invalidated the "grandfather clause,"
a law that effectively precluded most southern blacks from voting,
because their grandfathers, being slaves, were not eligible to vote.
In 1927 the organization won a Supreme Court case that began the
legal battle against the all-white primary.*

*From 1918 to 1955 the NAACP grew and spread across the
South, despite many uncoordinated attempts by white southerners
to stop its growth. About 1950 a coordinated attack against the
NAACP began throughout the South; this attack became highly
organized and effective from 1954 to 1956, then began to recede
about 1959.*

*The white power structure of the South decided to destroy the
southern operation of the NAACP by using legal tactics. The heads
of state governments called for special sessions of state legislatures,
and they decided that the NAACP should be required to make public
its membership lists. Charges that the organization was communistic
or subversive were used to justify this demand.*

*The NAACP refused to comply, and within a span of six
months in 1956 the attorney generals of Louisiana, Texas, and
Alabama obtained injunctions that stopped the operation of the
NAACP in their states. Other states took similar actions. The
legislature of South Carolina passed its law that barred teachers from
belonging to the NAACP, which made it possible for the Charleston
School Board to drop Mrs. Clark.*

*In 1955 the NAACP had 128,716 members in the southern
states, which represented 45 percent of its total membership. Two
years later membership in the South dropped to 79,677, only 28
percent of the total. Some interpreters argue that this coordinated
attack on the NAACP by white southern officials greatly contributed
to the emergence of the modern civil rights movement, since it cleared
the way for new mass movement organizations and encouraged
blacks to use the tactics of direct confrontation rather than relying
on the courts. For documentation of this interpretation, see chapters
one and two of Aldon D. Morris,* The Origins of the Civil Rights
Movement *(1984).*

Highlander and the First Citizenship School

AFTER I LOST MY JOB in Charleston, I was asked by Myles Horton to become the director of workshops at Highlander Folk School in Monteagle, Tennessee. When I moved there in June of 1956, I had already been going for two summers, so I knew what to expect.

The school was located on a farm fifty miles northeast of Chattanooga, Tennessee, out in the hills near a little town called Monteagle. Highlander had about 200 acres of land, rolling hills covered with trees there on the Cumberland Plateau. Eventually it had a main building and six others, plus about eight residences. About half of the total number of buildings were built after I came.

I lived upstairs in the wing of the main building. The library was underneath my rooms, which made them noisy and in the center of things. But I liked that. When a new stone residence was constructed out back behind the main building, Myles Horton offered me that, but I wouldn't take it. Blacks had always been put out back in the woods. I wanted to be up front where I could see and be seen.

Living at Highlander was no easy task for me. I had lots of things up there that were sort of detrimental to your health, if you'd let them be. But I had such a wonderful reception when I went around to the friends of Highlander in Cleveland, in New York City, in Philadelphia, that I just let all those other things pass me by.

Once I had my little granddaughter up there at Highlander, and she wanted an ice cream cone. We went to the drugstore in Monteagle, and bought a cone, which they served her. She sat up on the seat and turned all around licking it, but I had to take her out of there. They didn't want no black girl sitting up there eating no ice cream cone. They asked me to take her out. They wouldn't have her sit up there.

The only place I could go to church was up at a town called Sewanee. Up there I went to the church they had designed for seminarians to preach to the black people who worked on the grounds. The other churches in the town of Monteagle I could never go to. I simply couldn't go.

When I went down to that little bank at Sewanee, I couldn't get a thing done there. A white person had to vouch for a black person before the bank would do business with you. But I had a good friend down there. He was of Russian birth, and he used to teach at the college. I could always get him to vouch for me, otherwise they would not have given me any money for those checks. He had to go along with me and say that he knew me, especially since I was coming from Highlander.

But at Highlander I found out that black people weren't the only ones discriminated against. I found out that whites were against whites. The low-income whites were considered dirt under the feet of the wealthy whites, just like blacks were. I had to go to Highlander to find out that there was so much prejudice in the minds of whites against whites. I didn't dream—I thought that everything white was right. But I found differently. I found out that they had a lot of prejudice against each other.

Now let me tell about another great leader who came out of those workshops at Highlander. His name was Esau Jenkins. I knew him when he was a boy of fourteen and came to my school to learn how to read. All his life Esau devoted himself to improving conditions on Johns Island, and I helped him in any way I could, because I knew he was fighting a hard battle by himself on that island.

Johns Island is one of those sea islands around the harbor of Charleston. It was not connected to Charleston with roads until right after World War II. Before that, it took about nine hours to travel the fifteen miles from Charleston to Johns Island. You had to ride a gasoline launch through miles of creeks and swamps that were drained and filled by the tides. So the people had been very isolated for a long time.

After I came back from going to Highlander the first time, I decided that I should get Esau Jenkins to go. He had lots of excuses about not going to Highlander. He said, "Oh, I got big insurance to pay. Oh, I got my children going to school."

I said, "Well, that's all right. You won't have to spend any money up there. All you have to do is go."

Esau did get enthused then. We went up there and found out that many people could talk to him and give him help. We met Mrs. Ethyl Clyde of the Clyde Line Steamship. She was a daughter of that man whose ships came all the way up from Florida to New York and back again. She lived in Huntington, Long Island, and she was really interested in black people in the South. There was one way Esau could get some money to buy a building and to start teaching the black people of Johns Island.

The next time I went to Highlander we had a piece of car, I say. It was a $1200 car. Esau did the driving. I bought a car in 1951 when my sister learned to drive, but I never was able to drive. My sister said my mind was on so many meetings that I never could learn to drive. I believe it's true, because I was all the time steeped in meetings. I invested in quite a few cars, but I never drove one.

We took people from Johns Island every time we went to Highlander. It was real amusing the first time the women went. They took boxes of chicken. They weren't going to sit down and eat with white folks. Myles say, "That's all right. Just let them stay up in their rooms." By Thursday, when all the chicken had gone, they came down. They were glad to sit at the table and eat.

They learned that they could be with white people, but it was hard for them. One boy said that you couldn't even look at a white girl down on the islands. If you did, you'd better not smile and you'd better not say hello, because if you did the sheriff would be to your house and drag you out. That is the kind of life they had. When they came to Highlander, they found out that they could sleep in the room with a white boy, and the women could sleep in the room with white women. They sat and talked with each other; it was a real experience for them.

Myles Horton had been into Charleston three different times to try to get people to come up to Highlander, but he hadn't been able to get anybody to follow him. Now through Esau he had a way to reach people. Esau felt that Myles was a great man, and that was all the people on Johns Island needed. They loved Esau, and they knew that anybody he would bring to them would be somebody that they really liked.

IDA BERMAN

Esau Jenkins and Myles Horton discuss the Citizenship Schools on Johns Island, 1959.

One Christmas Myles went down there with his children and spent the whole Christmas season just walking around the island and talking. He stayed in Esau's house, and the people really enjoyed him.

Myles had a way of speaking to people which made them become endeared to him. He went to talk to some fellow who was overseer at one of the cabbage farms. We had the largest cabbage farms in the world on that place called Young's Island. Myles told this guy, "Now see, if you get people educated, you won't waste your cabbages. They'll learn how to cut cabbage closer, and you'll have more to sell."

Myles always told people about the injustices that were there, that they had not seen. He said, "Now, you know, any day I can go back with my own people and not have to endure these things, but you have to live with them always. I want you to see if you can get to the place where you can register and vote. After you've learned to read and write, you can become a person who will look into these things more and get to do more of it yourself. Then your children are coming along, and you need to think about what you need to do for these children, because they don't want to be living from hand to mouth like you have done all the time."

The people on Johns Island had a big parade for Myles Horton. They had him sitting up in a car riding through the roads with people on either side just yelling and screaming and praising Myles Horton. He didn't know how he felt.

About when Esau first came up to Highlander, he said to himself, "I think I should run for school board." He did, and he got 203 votes—all of the black people on Johns Island who had registered. But that wasn't enough to win, and it was only 18% of those who could be registered if they could read. That made him feel, "Now, I should try to get some more people registered, because then I would have more votes."

Esau had a wife and seven children to support. Being a small farmer was not enough, so Esau found a way to buy a bus. At first he transported school children, and later he drove his bus from Johns Island to Charleston and back, carrying tobacco workers and longshoremen to work.

One morning one of the women on the bus, as they were riding along toward Charleston, made Esau a proposal. "I don't have much schooling, Esau," she said to him. "I wasn't even able to get through the third grade. But I would like to be somebody. I'd like to hold up my head with other people; I'd like to be able to vote. Esau, if you'll help me a little when you have the time, I'll be glad to learn the laws and get qualified to vote. If I do, I promise you I'll register and I'll vote."

That appealed to Esau, and he agreed to help her. He had a portion of the South Carolina laws typed up, those that pertained to registration and voting, and he passed them out to the people who rode his bus. To those who couldn't read or couldn't understand the language of the law, he patiently explained the requirements. When he was waiting for his passengers to assemble or when his bus arrived in town a few minutes early, he would discuss those laws with them.

The woman who asked Esau for help was Mrs. Alice Wine. She had a marvelous ability to memorize; she memorized the whole section of the Constitution that they were studying. Soon she was ready to go and be registered.

While she was standing in line awaiting her turn, one of the women ahead of her, in reading a section of the constitution, mispronounced the word "miscegenation." Immediately Mrs. Wine pronounced it correctly. The registrar spoke out sharply, "No coaching, please!" When it came her time, Mrs. Wine "read" every word perfectly by reciting from memory. She was given her registration certificate, and she was one happy soul.

But Mrs. Wine wasn't satisfied. She really wanted to know how to read. She asked Esau if there was any kind of a school where she could learn to read and write.

There was no such school. Esau himself had very little education. I taught him to read when he was a teenager, but he was not equipped to teach others. His greatest qualification was his love of people and his determination to do all he could to help them.

Esau talked with me and discussed it with numerous others. He found that he couldn't get help from the local school. The principal was afraid to allow adults to come in to learn how to read and write in order to vote. He thought the school authorities might frown on that; he wasn't willing to risk it. He figured it might cost him his job.

Next Esau tried a preacher in the community. But the preacher's wife was teaching in the public school, and the preacher was afraid to let Esau use the Methodist Center as a meeting place for the adults' school. It could possibly cost the preacher's wife her job.

When Esau couldn't find a place to rent for a school, he asked me and Myles if Highlander could help. Highlander agreed to put up the money to buy a building. Esau's group bought a dilapidated school house for $1500. First it was going to sell for $1000, but when they found that blacks were going to use it, they asked $1500. We got it, and Esau's group fixed the front part like a grocery store and sold things to themselves. There were two rooms in the back part, and in those two rooms we taught.

We planned the grocery store to fool white people. We didn't want them to know that we had a school back there. We said we'd divide the thing into three parts. One part would be for the grocery store, and two rooms in back would be for the teaching. We didn't have any windows back there at that time, so white people couldn't peep in. That's the way we planned it.

We had about twenty-six people gathered together who were called the Progressive Club. Esau had organized this club before he went to Highlander, but now they had a store where they could sell items to themselves.

They decided that they would have to pay back the $1500 that Highlander paid for them, so that Highlander could pay the teacher who was going to teach. The profits from the sales did that. When they were through paying the $1500 back, they shared among themselves. Once there was a woman who got burned out, and they used all their profits to build her another house. They also used the profits for sickness and other things.

Next we had to find a teacher. I was directing the work at Highlander, and that work took me into so many different places that I would not have the time to do the day-by-day teaching. Besides going into the deep south states, holding meetings, getting people to realize that we should have Citizenship Schools, I was also going to the north, the midwest, and the west fund-raising for the Highlander Folk School.

We wanted to find a person who was not a licensed teacher, one who would not be considered high falutin, who would not act condescending to adults.

IDA BERMAN

The Citizenship School on Johns Island with teacher Septima Clark (center), Alice Wine (second from left), and Bernice Robinson (standing), January, 1959.

48

We decided we were going to ask Bernice Robinson to teach the first school for Esau. Bernice is a cousin of mine, and she'd been in New York for many years working as a beautician. When her mother became ill and her parents needed her, she decided to move back to Charleston. Then I decided that I was going to try to take Bernice with me up to Highlander, which I did. When she went up there and found the type of people that we had, southern whites and northern whites, southern blacks and northern blacks, all living and working together, she decided that she should try to do something herself.

Now the people on Johns Island knew me, so I went down first and introduced them to Bernice. But Bernice had already been working with Esau Jenkins, who was one of them. They had worked together on voter registration drives for the NAACP. When you can work through "one of them," as they say, you can get the real feeling from them that you're somebody that they can trust. Esau could be trusted on the island, and because he could be trusted, he could introduce us to numbers of others who would trust us. People on the island didn't want to trust black people coming from the city. They just thought that you were so high-falutin that you were going to try to make fun of them.

Bernice say, "I'm a beautician. I don't know anything about teaching."

But Myles and I believed she could do it. We knew that she had the most important quality, the ability to listen to people.

Bernice had two sisters-in-law who were teaching in the early grades, and she got some teaching materials from them. When she went in on the first night, she carried that grade school material and a voter registration application.

Bernice realized right away that the grade school material was too juvenile. Just facing those adults, she realized she couldn't use it. She told them that she was not really their teacher, but that they were going to learn together. She would teach them some things, and they were going to teach her a lot more.

All Bernice had to use was that voter registration form. She called each person up to the table to read lines from the form; then she asked them each to write their name in cursive. That's how she found out where they were in reading and writing.

They told Bernice the first thing they wanted to learn was how to write their name in cursive. She had them practice on posterboard so they wouldn't press their pencils through. They had to do it in cursive because printing didn't count for signing checks. They kept tracing over their names until they got the swing of it.

They had lots of trouble holding their pencils. One man I taught later on, Rev. John Smalls, bored through his paper I guess a hundred times or more. Now he'd been used to a plow, and the pencil was too light. Finally I got him to the place where he could hold a pencil and write his name. But it was quite a task. It took a little time.

Bernice and her students would tell stories about the things they had to deal with every day—about growing vegetables, plowing the land, digging up potatoes. Then they would write down these stories and read them back. Any word they stumbled over, Bernice would use in the spelling lesson.

When the people told Bernice they wanted to learn how to fill out a money order, she got one from the post office and traced it onto posterboard so they could practice.

After they could read a little bit, Bernice worked with them on the election laws and the parts of the Constitution that they would have to read to the registrar.

When I finally had time to visit Bernice's class, it was already the last week of the two-month session. Classes were held in January and February because that was the laying by season. The men were out of the fields; they couldn't have come when they were in the fields.

Bernice asked me to teach that class so she could see how I would do it. I took words out of the Constitution and divided each word into syllables and practiced pronouncing them. Then we discussed together the meaning of each word until we all understood what they meant. Bernice was shocked. She had been teaching exactly the same way, but until then we hadn't talked about it with each other.

That first class had fourteen people in it—three men and eleven women. Some of the women brought their teenage girls because they couldn't leave them at home alone. They wanted to learn to crochet and sew, and Bernice taught them. She even got a sewing machine for them.

The next year the class met in December, January and February. By then people were really registering well and fast, because the ones in the class were influencing others who could already read and write to go in to register. We started another class on the next island, Wadmalaw, taught by Esau's daughter. Soon we had five schools going on the islands, and Bernice was supervising all of them.

After Bernice had been teaching there for three years, a white fellow from Charleston came around. Bernice said she saw him peeping around. He found out that blacks were learning to read, and he went back and told it to the media. *The Charleston Evening Post* and *The News and Courier* printed, "There's a school on the island. Not a White Citizens' Council, not a Ku Klux Klan, none of us knew about this school. They're teaching Negroes to read, and teaching them to register and to vote. We didn't know one thing that was happening, and we just found this out."

After I read that, I went over there to see how the blacks were taking it. I saw one man on the porch of a store reading this article to the others around, so I said, "How do you feel about it?"

He answered, "Oh, anytime that white people think that we are getting something done, they're going to be against us. We're going ahead with our school and do this thing."

I said, "Well, that's good. We don't have any trouble here." We were able to get that over. No one got punished at all. I went from one island to another where we had schools, and I found that the black people weren't afraid anymore.

I, too, learned not to be afraid anymore. I never dreamed that I could speak my mind to a white man until I got up

Discussion of voting on Edisto Island, 1959.

there at Highlander with Myles Horton. While we were trying
to plan for the Citizenship Education Program, Myles thought
we could just go into communities and get people registered
to vote. But I knew that these people had had no schooling,
because according to U.S. statistics we had 12 million illiter-
ates in the South. If they were illiterate, with the laws that
we had, they would not be able to read enough to register
in most southern states.

Myles thought I could go right into the community and
get a large group of people, talk to them, and then bring
them up to the registration booth and get them registered.
You can do that now, because the laws have changed, but

then black people had to read. From the office at Highlander we sent to all of those states for election laws. Myles hadn't read them. He was just making a guess of what you could do. But when we looked through these election laws, we knew what we had do with those people. We had to get them trained to read those laws and answer those questions.

So Myles and I had to just shout it out. That's what we did—shouted at each other. Finally I got to the place where I could put down on paper what I felt would be good for the first night, what would be a good beginning the next morning, how the meals should be served, how to get buses to transport people, and how we would have to have money for all those things.

But it was hard for Myles to see me saying things of that type. Finally, we hit on the plan that was right, but we weren't doing too good at first. Myles would ask me about methods, and I would say, "Don't ask me about methods. Let me tell you how I'm going to do this thing." Myles would go back home and think about what I said; then he would come back the next day and get things typed up the way I suggested. This is what we did.

People thought I had new-fangled ideas. Myles thought I had new-fangled ideas. But my new-fangled ideas worked out. I didn't know they were going to work out though. I just thought that you couldn't get people to register and vote until you teach them to read and write. That's what I thought, and I was so right.

But I changed, too, as I traveled through the eleven deep south states. Working through those states, I found I could say nothing to those people, and no teacher as a rule could speak with them. We had to let them talk to us and say to us whatever they wanted to say. When we got through listening to them, we would let them know that we felt that they were right according to the kind of thing that they had in their mind, but according to living in this world there were other things they needed to know. We wanted to know if they were willing then to listen to us, and they decided that they wanted to listen to us.

But I had to change, too, because I used to feel that whatever was white was right, and it took many years of working before I could feel that they were not exactly right, as I thought they were. As the change came to me, I was able to get that change over to others. Because I had grown up with a very strong disciplined mother, who felt that whatever she had in her mind was right, so I felt that whatever I had in my mind was right, too. I found out that I needed to change my way of thinking, and in changing my way of thinking I had to let people understand that their way of thinking was not the only way. We had to work together to get the changes.

Raid on Highlander

LOTS OF WHITE PEOPLE considered Highlander a Communist place. One way this idea got started was on account of the fact that the editor of *The News and Courier* in Charleston had a son up at Sewanee going to school. The editor went up there to see his son and came down to visit Myles two or three times. We had meetings there, and he talked with us. He looked at Myles' house, and he declared that the flat roof was built that way so helicopters from Russia could come in and tell the people how to become part of the Russian communistic group. This is what he said in his paper and that gave us that kind of publicity.

But anyone who was against segregation was considered a Communist. White southerners couldn't believe that a southerner could have the idea of racial equality; they thought it had to come from somewhere else.

Highlander had been called a hotbed of Communist activity for a long time—way back into the 1930s. But this charge really got going in 1957, when Highlander celebrated its twenty-fifth anniversary. We got Rev. Martin Luther King, Jr., to be our main speaker for that anniversary. While he was at Highlander, the governor of Georgia sent an undercover agent to the celebration to find out what was going on. At the same time a Communist newspaper, *The Daily Worker,* sent a columnist, who didn't let on who he was either. Well, that agent for the Governor of Georgia took a picture of Rev. King sitting in an integrated audience near the columnist from *The Daily Worker.* Don't you know, that picture was made into a billboard and plastered all over the South as "proof" that Rev. King had attended "a Communist training center."

After that the state of Tennessee decided to investigate "the subversive activities" of Highlander Folk School. The legislature held some hearings; then it asked the district attorney general to bring a suit against Highlander to revoke its charter.

The district attorney had to figure out what charge he could use to shut Highlander down. It was really Highlander's integration that the state wanted to stop, but they didn't want to go to court on that. The U.S. Supreme Court had already ruled that segregation in schools was unconstitutional, and Tennessee might lose its case on that issue.

The district attorney thought up another charge. He knew that Highlander's charter did not permit anything to be sold on its premises. It did not have a license to sell drinks or anything.

Now the men who came to the workshops at Highlander liked to drink beer. But the black men couldn't go up into the village and buy beer. The storekeepers wouldn't sell to black people. I was the only black person living in Grundy County.

The men solved that problem by putting their money together at Highlander, then the white men would go buy the beer and put it in a cooler at the school, where everybody could go and take a bottle and drink it.

When I was director of the educational program at Highlander, they didn't have any beer. That's one thing I spoke about with Myles. The men did like to drink beer, but I felt as if we didn't need to have the beer, because I saw quite a few of the union men that the beer made almost crazy. They didn't act like themselves. Some of them couldn't get out of bed to come to the workshop the next day, and I didn't want to be wrestling with people with beer. When Myles had to go to Europe on a trip, I certainly put my foot down that I was not going to have any beer-selling.

Myles had to go to Europe in the summer of 1959. He left me in charge of the program at Highlander. While he was away, on July 31, about eighteen Tennessee police officers under the direction of the District Attorney made a raid on

Highlander. I was leading a workshop, and that night we were showing a movie, "The Face of the South," made by George Mitchell.

When it got to the place where George Mitchell was saying in this movie, "They went to the schools that we gave them, which weren't very good," the police burst in and said, "Put that film out."

One of the girls said, "You have arrested Septima Clark, and we don't know how to turn this thing off."

He jerked the plug out of the wall, while one of the teenagers made up a new verse to "We Shall Overcome." She started singing, and everyone followed: "We are not afraid, we are not afraid tonight."

He say, "You can sing, but don't sing too loud." They had numbers of verses to it, and they sang them all. It made the police feel nervous.

The police were looking for some excuse to close down Highlander. The big trouble was its integration, but they didn't want to say that. So they claimed they were searching for whiskey. They didn't find any. I said to them, when they came to me: "Just go in that kitchen and look all over. You won't even find cooking sherry in there." It was so funny.

The young man who was living in Myles' house at the time gave them the key to his house. That's how they got into Myles' house and went down into the cellar and found the demijohn there. That's one of those covered jugs, all full of cobwebs and everything, and they put enough moonshine in it so that it would satisfy the state that we were selling moonshine. That is what they did.

That night I should have been afraid because they carried me around the mountain and then put me into another car. Then they went around another mountain. I thought, "Now I don't know whether I'll get to see the daylight or not." They felt that the black people in the workshop would follow them. I didn't feel too good riding with them, because I do know that those young mountain boys had beaten others to death, and I had a feeling that that might happen to me. One of the white students who was arrested along with me started talking back to the man. I said "You're just as bad as they are if you're going to do that," because I didn't want them to start beating us.

In the jail I asked them could I use a telephone. They said, "Oh, no." But I knew I had the right to use a telephone. You can always use it once, and I was going to call a lawyer in Nashville. But they weren't going to let me do that.

They put me in this room, and there were men above me. Whenever they used the toilet, all the stuff came right down through my room. This is the way it was. I had to sit up there, and the only thing I could think of was I'd sing, "Michael, Row the Boat Ashore." We had had a workshop, and Harry Belafonte had been there, teaching us "Michael Row." So I just sat up there and sang that, until they came to get me out of that room.

I didn't have to wait until the bank opened in the morning to get out of jail. Two white teachers who had come to the mountains to teach kept $500 in cash under their bed. When they heard I was in jail, they came down that night and put up the $500 bail so I could get out.

Anyway, we went through that, and lots of people were terribly afraid. The little town of Sewanee had a Western Union office, and when it came out in the papers that I was arrested, there were hundreds of telegrams coming to that little office. A woman in Columbia, South Carolina, had a son teaching up there at Sewanee, and she told him not to phone, but to come down there and see what was happening. She wanted to know if I were safe.

When he got there, my granddaughter and I were sitting up on the front of that little house just as if nothing had happened. I wasn't at all worried. I was back, and I finished up the workshop and sent the people on their way. That night some young white men came, and I was taking soiled sheets off the beds, throwing them down the steps so that the laundry man would get them the next day. They just laughed and screamed names at me and went on about their business.

Of course, I got lots of dirty phone calls, calling me all kinds of things. But it didn't scare me out of that house. I was living there alone after the workshop people left, just with my little granddaughter. The maintenance man at Highlander became nervous. Although he was a Monteagle man, he decided he couldn't stay there any longer, and he moved his family down to Florida somewhere.

When we had the trial in the early fall, not any of them could testify that I was selling liquor. They didn't see anything like that. Some of them testified that they hated Highlander because black people were coming there dressed up, looking better than they were. Some of them testified that they saw black women and white men going into various houses, which really wasn't true, and they couldn't prove it.

The judge said when he was sentencing us that the evidence said that we were having liquor sold there at the school, so he had to put a padlock on the door. But he felt as if all the things that were said were not true. He said that himself.

A reporter from Chattanooga said in *The Chattanooga Observer*, "I've never seen a woman so harassed on a witness stand before, but she took it well." He was talking about me.

I wasn't going to let them scare me to death. I just wouldn't let them. But it wasn't an easy thing, because when you'd go home you would keep thinking what they could do and what they might do, because they were very, very harassing and very mean, very much so.

All Over the Deep South

THE RAID ON HIGHLANDER did not stop us from continuing our program. We set up workshops to train teachers to go out and set up Citizenship Schools. By the spring of 1961 eighty-two teachers who had received training at Highlander were holding classes in Alabama, Georgia, South Carolina, and Tennessee.

I traveled by bus all over the South, visiting those teachers and recruiting new ones. I always took the fifth seat from the front to test the buses. They asked me to move, but I didn't. I reminded them that we had a law now that said we could sit anywhere in the bus. I had six pieces of luggage because I was carrying teaching materials and films to show, and the porters always put my luggage to the back of the bus. They assumed that is where I would sit, but I didn't.

In addition to training the teachers, I was fund-raising for Highlander. I traveled by plane all over the north, the midwest, and the far west, staying in the homes of friends of Highlander.

In January of 1961 I had my second heart attack. The first one took place at Highlander four years earlier during a workshop with some women from Montgomery. I stayed in the hospital four days with that one—the first time a black person had ever been in the Sewanee hospital.

My second heart attack took place in Charleston. We were immunizing children, and we couldn't get the white nurses to push up the sleeves of the black children and rub their arms. I was going to the library to talk about it with a doctor who had his office on the floor above the library. I had lots on my mind. A white woman who had come to help with the shots was staying at my house, and I knew my mother was very worried about that.

When I got to the top of those steps, I sat down and couldn't go any further. I got back down the steps, and the librarian took me to the colored hospital. I did not feel too worried after the doctor said that it was not one of those extreme heart attacks. All they wanted me to do was to try to lie down and rest. I stayed there nearly two weeks just resting.

People at Highlander were nervous about my health; they felt that I was overworked. Myles decided to ask Bernice Robinson to come down and work at Highlander to help me train teachers for those Citizenship Schools.

During the summer of 1961 we saw that we needed to move our citizenship program away from Highlander, in order to keep it going even if the state of Tennessee shut down Highlander. By that time Myles and I knew Dr. Martin Luther King, Jr., who was then president of the Southern Christian Leadership Conference, or SCLC as we called it.

SCLC grew out of Rosa Park's refusal to stand up on the bus. After the bus boycott in Montgomery had been won, the idea of non-violent resistance spread. Black people needed an organization to co-ordinate their efforts across the South. So SCLC was formally organized in New Orleans in March, 1957, with Dr. King as president.

After the raid on Highlander in July of 1959, Dr. King and Myles Horton got together to see if they could use the program that we had already planned, and they decided they could. Andy Young came to SCLC at that time, sent by the United Church of Christ in New York. It was agreed to open up a place and train people to go into the South to work. Then the Marshall Field Foundation fund was transferred to SCLC, and Dr. King said that he would like for me to come along with the funds.

So I went to Atlanta. I stayed in Atlanta on the weekends; on Monday morning I would get into a car and be driven somewhere in the South. I would stay for a week or two, trying to get people to want to have Citizenship Schools or helping with protests and marches.

But let me go back and tell you now I met Martin Luther King, Jr. The State Department sent a woman from Nigeria, Mrs. Io Dele, and I had to accompany her from Highlander to Atlanta. She was looking at social work in this country, to see how we cared for people. I got in touch with a social worker in Atlanta, and I was to deliver Mrs. Io Dele to her. Being with a Nigerian princess, I got a lot of good flak. Going on the plane I had people running—you know, here comes this Nigerian princess, and here I was behind her. After I got to Atlanta Dr. King was there, and so I got to meet him.

We worked about two years getting him to come for our twenty-fifth anniversary at Highlander, and we did get him to come. That's when I was really able to talk with him and know him. I was doing some workshop sessions then, and that's when he got to know of the work that I could do. That's when he decided, since we were being closed out, that he wanted me to come to Atlanta and work with the Southern Christian Leadership Conference.

SCLC never paid me directly. Under the terms of their incorporation, they could not receive grants from foundations. But I worked for them through the United Church of Christ in New York City. Andrew Young arranged that because he was working for that church. That's where the funds went, and those were the people who paid my salary when I worked at SCLC.

The United Church of Christ owned a center in Liberty County, Georgia. We asked the man in charge in New York through Andy Young if we could use that center. They used to have some kind of a school there, but it had been closed for quite some time. We were able to get that center, and we could hire people in the community to do the cooking, make the beds and get the place ready for us. That center was called the Dorchester Cooperative Community Center in McIntosh, Georgia, some 295 miles from Atlanta and forty miles south of Savannah.

Three of us from SCLC drove all over the South recruiting people to go to the Dorchester Center. Andy Young was the administrator, Dorothy Cotton was the director or the educational consultant, and I was the supervisor of teacher training. The three of us worked together as a team, and we drove all over the South bringing busloads of folk—sometimes seventy people—who would live together for five days at the Dorchester Center.

Once a month, for five days, we'd work with the people we had recruited, some of whom were just off the farms. Like Fannie Lou Hamer, who stood up and said, "I live on Mr. Marlowe's plantation." She talked about how Pap, her husband, had to take her to the next county because they were going to beat up Pap and her if she didn't stop that voter registration talk. She taught us the old songs that they sang in the meetings to keep their spirits up. We sang a lot in the workshops at Dorchester, just like at Highlander.

We went into various communities and found people who could read well aloud and write legibly. They didn't have to have a certificate of any kind. I sat down and wrote out a flyer saying that the teachers we need in a Citizenship School should be people who are respected by the members of the community, who can read well aloud, and who can write their names in cursive writing. These are the ones that we looked for.

We brought those people to the center in Liberty County, Georgia. While they were there, we gave them the plan for teaching in a citizenship school. We had a day-by-day plan, which started the first night with them talking, telling us what they would like to learn. The next morning we started off with asking them: "Do you have an employment office in your town? Where is it located? What hours is it open? Have you been there to get work?"

The answers to those things we wrote down on dry cleaner's bags, so they could read them. We didn't have any blackboards. That afternoon we would ask them about the government in their home town. They knew very little about it. They didn't know anything about the policemen or the mayor or anything like that. We had to give them a plan of how these people were elected, of how people who had registered to vote could put these people in office, and of how they were the ones who were over you.

We were trying to make teachers out of these people who could barely read and write. But they could teach. If they could read at all, we could teach them that c-o-n-s-t-i-t-u-t-i-o-n spells constitution. We'd have a long discussion all morning about what the constitution was. We were never telling anybody. We used a very non-directive approach.

The people who left Dorchester went home to teach and to work in voter registration drives. They went home, and they didn't take it anymore. They started their own citizenship classes, discussing the problems in their own towns. "How come the pavement stops where the black section begins?" Asking questions like that, and then knowing who to go to talk to about that, or where to protest it.

The first night at the Liberty County Center we would always ask people to tell the needs of the people in their community. The first night they gave us their input, and the next morning we started teaching from what they wanted to do.

But what they wanted varied. We had to change. Down in the southern part of Georgia some women wanted to know how to make out bank checks. One woman told the workshop that somebody had been able to withdraw a lot of money from her account because she did not know how to make out her own check and check up on her own account. She was in the habit of having someone white make out her check for her, and then she'd sign with an "X."

So we started teaching banking. We brought in a banker, and he put the whole form up on the board and showed them how to put in the date and how to write it out. He told them, "Don't leave a space at the end of the check. Somebody else could write another number in there. When you finish putting down the amount, take a line and carry it all the way to the dollar mark."

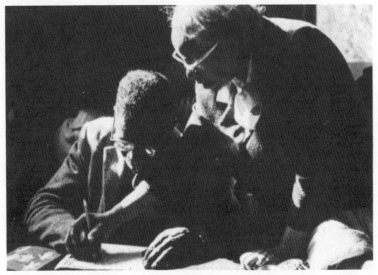

SCLC's Citizenship Education Program in Camden, Alabama, 1966.

He was very good, but the white people in Liberty County got to the place where they were against his coming to teach. When they found out that black people were learning to write their names, they got very angry about it. One night we had a whole group of white farmers out there against us. They were cursing, but they didn't shoot. The banker got away; he got in his car and drove on back to his town.

There was a good side to that, too. When black people learned how to withdraw their money from the banks, they went to merchants to buy new clothes. Then the merchants were happy that they had some money.

The Marshall Field Foundation gave us a $250,000 grant. With that money we gave the students $30 to come to school two nights a week, two hours a night, for three months at a time. They were always in debt. We felt that if they didn't make anything on the farm, we had to pay them.

Even then we didn't have too many to come. There was so much pressure from the whites in the community that too many of them were afraid. Those who came had to feel that we could get away with it or that we didn't mind if we had to die.

65

Black people in small southern towns didn't trust black people coming in from the city. They just thought that you were so high falutin that you were going to try to make fun of them. I found out when I went into small communities that the illiterate blacks in these communities were ashamed to let me know that they were illiterate. I had to walk around and get people in that community to believe in what I wanted done.

Here is an example of what I did when I went into a new town. This is what happened when I went to Huntsville, Alabama. I decided to go there because in Cincinnati, Ohio, I met a Jewish rabbi who had a group of Jewish people in Huntsville that he was trying to work with. They told him of the injustices that the blacks had and the fact that they could not register to vote. I came home to tell Myles about it, and he gave me the name of a woman, a Miss Harris, who ran an orphan house in Huntsville.

I went over there to see Miss Harris. I brought two of her daughters back to Highlander with me, so they could get the feel of it. When they got ready to go home I went with them, and I stayed with them for some time. Miss Harris was busy getting her place together with her orphan children, and I contributed $15 on a frigidaire that she needed, which spelled a lot. She introduced me to a black minister, a Baptist minister. I went to his house, and we sat and talked. We walked around approximately two weeks, just talking and talking to people. Finally I got him to invite ten other persons, a Methodist minister along, to have luncheon with us. I paid for the luncheon, too. I had money from Highlander to do these things.

At that luncheon meeting I told them about the Citizenship Schools. I told this Methodist minister that I would like very much for him to do some teaching for me and that he could come to a workshop with me—just spend a weekend, and he could see the program that we had. He came, but when I went to his church, he had too many middle-class black teachers who worked at a college in Huntsville so that it was no way in the world that I could get them to do anything whatsoever. They were too scared. When I went to his church that Sunday, he introduced me, but he wouldn't mention Citizenship Schools.

Nevertheless, I kept talking around and working with them until we were able to set up three schools in Huntsville. I let them know that the people who taught would be paid some money for their time. Those things were the drawing cards for the people as they went along.

The teachers received $75 a month after we brought them to the Liberty County Center and taught them how to teach others. When I was in Selma, a young woman got her check for $75. She said, "I've never had this much money in my life." She was very happy over it.

All of the states had different election laws. Georgia had thirty questions, and people who wanted to register had to answer twenty-four out of thirty. Alabama had about twenty-four questions they had to answer. One of them was: "Give the definition of a thief." One teacher said she never could give the definition because the registrar wanted her to say, "A thief is a nigger who steals." Because she couldn't say that, or didn't know that she should say that, she never could pass.

Of course, we didn't teach them to say a thief is a nigger who steals. We kept working on that question, "What is a thief?" and we found definitions out of the dictionary. One woman said she said, "Well, the dictionary says this." And the registrar said, "Well, maybe it does, but that's not what we want," and she was refused her registration.

I have to laugh when I think of those people. I wonder if they think about themselves, how silly they were making those kinds of laws.

There was a fellow at Tuskegee Institute in Alabama who had his Ph.D. He read the Constitution too well, so they gave him some Chinese to read. He couldn't get his registration certificate either. In Louisiana even the women had to say, "I am not the father of an illegitimate child."

To try to get around that problem of answering the questions to the satisfaction of the registrar, an organization was formed in Tuskegee. Someone went to Washington two or three times to talk with the U.S. Attorney General. That little organization used about $1300 sending people back and forth to Washington. Finally, the people in Washington would phone down to the registering group to let them know it was against the laws of the United States to ask people to give definitions according to the satisfaction of the registrar.

But the whites in Tuskegee tried everything. When they saw the black people coming in to register at the bank, the registrar would hide in a vault and pretend that registration was closed. We had a lady there who was very fair; they couldn't tell whether she was black or white. We sent her in, and when the man came out to register her, the other black people surged in. He said, "Oh, my God. Here comes the niggers." They thought they had a white woman, but she was one of us.

In the summer of 1965 Congress passed the Voting Rights Act, which eliminated all literacy tests. After that, people in Alabama did not have to answer twenty-four questions. They could register to vote if they could sign their name in cursive. It didn't take us but twenty minutes in Selma, Alabama, to teach a woman to write her name. The white students took her to the courthouse. She wrote her name in cursive writing and came back with a number that meant she could register to vote. This is the way we did it.

We had 150 of those schools in Selma, paying those teachers $1.25 an hour, two hours each morning, five days a week. The Marshall Field Foundation furnished the money for that, and we did it for three solid months. At the end of three months, we had 7002 persons with a number that gave them the right to vote when the federal man came down in August. We worked from May 18 to August 15. That was in 1965, because in 1966 we went to the vote.

The black ministers in Selma were just as bad as the middle-class teachers in Huntsville. When the ministers had an anniversary, they would get a suit from the merchants up town. So they didn't want us to teach those people how to write their names. Dr. King sent in a team of five of us to do that teaching, and I was the only one who stayed for those three months. The rest of them left me because they got angry with the black preachers. Then I trained others to help me do the work.

The black preachers would say, "Who's going to pay for this? Who's going to do so-and-so?" Back of it was the fact that they didn't want the white people to know that we were teaching blacks to write their names, for then the merchants would stop giving the preachers their anniversary gifts. They wanted those gifts. Material things were more to them than the human value things.

But I toughed it out with those men. I met one day with five of them, and they said, "Who's going to pay for it?" I said, "We'll pay the teachers." They said, "Who's going to advertise it?" I said, "Well, I'll get the advertising done. I'll go around to the churches." At one o'clock in the morning I was going through Selma hunting up preachers to make that announcement the next day. It was something.

Of course, I understand those preachers. I know they were dependent on white people's approval. Even with their congregation's support, they could be run out of town if the white power structure decided they ought to go. Often they weren't against the Movement; they were just afraid to join it openly. It's simply a contradiction: so many preachers supported the Movement that we can say it was based in churches, yet many preachers couldn't take sides with it because they thought they had too much to lose.

In Selma, anybody who came to our meeting lost their job. Fifty or more did. Some of them got their jobs back later, but some never did. I couldn't stay at any of their houses because the whites knew me so well they would have harassed anyone I stayed with. I had to rent a room in a motel. Dr. King had to send money from the SCLC to buy groceries for the people who lost their jobs.

But even with this kind of harassment, the Citizenship Schools really got into full force. There were 897 going from 1957 to 1970. In 1964 there were 195 going at one time. They were in people's kitchens, in beauty parlors, and under trees in the summertime. I went all over the South, sometimes visiting three Citizenship Schools in one day, checking to be sure they weren't using textbooks, but were teaching people to read those election laws and to write their names in cursive writing.

One time I heard Andy Young say that the Citizenship Schools were the base on which the whole civil rights movement was built. And that's probably very much true.

It's true because the Citizenship Schools made people aware of the political situation in their area. We recruited the wise leaders of their communities, like Fannie Lou Hamer in Mississippi. Hosea Williams started out as a Citizenship School Supervisor. The Citizenship School classes formed the grassroot basis of new statewide political organizations in South Carolina, Georgia, and Mississippi. From one end of the South to the other, if you look at the black elected officials and the political leaders, you find people who had their first involvement in the training program of the Citizenship School.

It was 1962 before the major civil rights groups were ready to do something about voter registration. But we had developed the ideas of the Citizenship Schools between 1957 and 1961. So all the civil rights groups could use our kind of approach, because by then we knew it worked.

In 1962 the SCLC joined four other groups—the Congress of Racial Equality (CORE), the NAACP, the Urban League, and the Student Non-Violent Coordinating Committee (SNCC)—to form the Voter Education Project. In the next four years all the groups together trained about 10,000 teachers for Citizenship Schools. During this period almost 700,000 black voters registered across the South. After the Voting Rights Act passed in 1965, registration increased very rapidly. At least a million more black people registered by 1970. But it took until the election of 1972 for the first two blacks from the Deep South to be elected to U.S. Congress since Reconstruction. They were Andrew Young, who helped me set up all those Citizenship Schools, and Barbara Jordan, from Texas.

Non-Violent Resistance

BUT BEFORE WE COULD SEND anyone to Congress, the white people tried some of everything. When we went down into Jackson, Mississippi, the mayor was a man named Thompson. He had a tank at the end of the street where we had to pass to register to vote. It was called "Thompson's Tank," there to shoot you as you passed by. But somehow or other we went by. We would usually kneel down and pray in front of the guns, and Thompson's tank didn't get to kill any of us.

But I never once felt afraid, not on any of those marches. Bullets could have gotten me, but somehow or other they didn't. I felt very good about going, about talking to people. I knew that people had gotten to the place where they saw the type of meanness that was being shown throughout their little towns. They hadn't noticed it before, but now they were ready from within to do something about it.

Whenever we had meetings, we would always have hard times. The White Citizens' Council or the Ku Klux Klan would be surrounding us wherever we were. In Marion, Alabama, one of the policemen there was about to slap the mother of this fellow named Jackson. He ran up to put his arms around his mother, and they shot him in the groin. He died the next day. We lost thirty people, from northern Virginia to eastern Texas, during the time we were working in the civil rights movement trying to get people registered.

But we still wanted them to work non-violently. In April, 1963, I went to Birmingham when the SCLC decided to hold demonstrations in that city. The police there were known to be very repressive and sure enough, Chief "Bull" Connors had his men turn fire hoses on the non-violent demonstrators. That was put on TV and got the sympathy of the rest of the country like nothing else had.

I worked with the students in Birmingham. Sometimes they wanted to fight back. I said to them: "Do you think you can take the slaps? Because they will slap your face or they will knock you down. Do you think you can take it? If you can, and turn around and move on or go to jail, all well and good. If you can't, don't go down. Stay up in this room with me." I was teaching them to be non-violent, and I had no idea whatsoever of feeling that some of them might be killed.

Working with those young white women who came down from the North was not easy either. They'd be not listening and almost running into trouble. I'd say, "Don't go out to nights in the streets because these folk don't know you, and they have a terrible feeling against Yankees anyhow. They see you out there, they're going to try to beat you, both blacks and whites. You better try to stop."

But they would sneak out at night. They'd want to go see the town. They had to run back most of the times and get into that house and lock those doors to keep them from coming in on them. They'd tell me about it the next day. I'd say, "Well, I tried to tell you not to go out at night. It's bad enough to try to go in the day, you know."

But it was nice that they came down to help us with that registration in Selma, Alabama. They had a lot of spunk, some of them, especially those who went into Mississippi. Mississippi did kill three, two whites, Andrew Goodman and Michael Schwerner, and one black boy, James Chaney. But the bulk of them weren't killed in Mississippi, not at all.

In Greenwood, Mississippi, a white fellow picked up a 15-year-old black boy and threw him down to the ground three times and broke his left leg in one or two places. We had to take him all the way to Clarksville, Mississippi, before he could get into a hospital. But people from all over the United States sent money to SCLC to help that boy.

The Sunday night after that happened I was in a Baptist

church in Granada, Mississippi. We were talking about registration and voting; Monday we were going to show them how to fill in these blanks. Just as we finished up that meeting and walked out of church, it caught fire in every corner. We didn't know how they got in to put those things in the various corners of that church, but that whole sanctuary just caught fire and started burning. We were just standing out in the street looking at it. We hadn't been out of there five minutes before the whole thing was going down. This just shows how mean people can be. The next night we had another meeting in the education building of that same church, and the next day I left to go to another part of Mississippi.

Traveling with Dr. King, I got to see how he personally reacted to violence. When that Nazi walked up on that platform in Birmingham and slapped Dr. King in his face three times, all the old men on crutches came up with their sticks to fight back. Dr. King put up his hand and said, "No, we mustn't fight. We have to pray for him."

Dr. King took the man downstairs in the basement of that hall we were in and asked him, "Didn't you know that you might have been killed in here?"

The Nazi replied, "Yes, but I have my beliefs just like you have yours, and if you're going to die for yours, I would die for mine."

Another time we were coming from Albany, Georgia, going to Atlanta, and Dr. King was in the front seat of the car with the driver. There were three of us sitting in the back seat going back after a meeting. A car full of white fellows came up. They zigzagged all in front of us. Finally, they tried to run us into a ditch. They pulled their car across the road, and the driver of our car got out, went into the back of our car, and pulled out a pistol. Then they went on.

Dr. King said, "Frank, did you think that I want you to do that? Oh, no. I don't want you to save me with a gun. We're fighting a non-violent fight. This is what I want."

The next time we went to Charleston for a meeting, Dr. King was way up in the tower of this building on a television show. He looked down and saw a row of six Nazis sitting in the front row. He say, "I bet they have me now." But they didn't. When he was through with his television interview, they took him out of a back door. He escaped that time, but those men were there, ready for a showdown. We kept that non-violent spirit regardless.

Stokely Carmichael was going through various towns in Alabama trying to get the young people to become what he called Black Power Boys. Dr. King felt that was just the opposite of what he was trying, so he invited Stokely Carmichael to come to his house one Sunday and have dinner with him. Stokely went, and Dr. King tried to impress upon him the idea that he should try to get these young people to become non-violent.

Well, Stokely went right out that next Monday on Auburn Avenue and had a lot of black boys with sticks smashing the windows of black merchants who failed to support Dr. King in his non-violent message.

Then I decided that I would try to convince Stokely. I invited him to meet me at a restaurant. I was going to give him dinner because I was boarding myself. He came and brought six boys with him to have dinner with me. I had them all seated and fed them all. Then I sat and talked with him about his idea of non-violence. I said, "Don't you think it would be so much better if you would have the city people give these boys the going rate to clean up Auburn Avenue, rather than have them break out the merchants' glasses because they didn't agree with Dr. King's non-violent message?"

Stokely just laughed. He really didn't think well of my ideas, and some of the fellows with him were just hee-hawing at me for saying that. Anyway, he was able to organize numbers of young people to become Black Power Boys. They gave the salute with the fist, upholding the fist with the thumb placed in the forefingers and saying, "Black Power! Black Power!"

I didn't get to see Stokely Carmichael anymore for quite some time. I met him next in Washington when I went to the Martin Luther King Center there. When he saw me coming in, he said: "There's Mrs. Clark. Stand up, Mrs. Clark.

74

She was the one who got me to realize that being violent was the one thing that I shouldn't do."

I felt that the Black Power Boys really didn't have the right idea. They thought that by violence they would be able to change things. But I thought, like Dr. King, that we would be able to become non-violent, and in our non-violent way we would disobey the laws they made. We wouldn't fight, but we would kneel down and pray about it. We would let the judges and legislators know we thought the law was wrong, and in that way we would be able to get many changes.

I could understand why Stokely felt so angry. He worked with the Student Non-Violent Coordinating Committee (SNCC) in Lowndes County, Alabama, registering people to vote. The whites in that area tried all kinds of crude violence, and Stokely was arrested about thirty-five times. So he and others in SNCC came to feel that black people had to take more initiative. Stokely and his friends made SNCC an all-black organization and gave up on non-violence. I don't believe they really wanted open violent attacks on whites, but at the very least they wanted blacks to defend themselves.

I had another chance to talk to the younger leaders about non-violence about the time Stokely was president of SNCC. In 1967 I went to the National Conference for New Politics in Chicago. It was supposed to build a coalition of college activists and black civil rights people, but the people there split into factions that could hardly talk to each other. The northern blacks, new to the movement, were fighting mad at all whites.

Most of the people at the conference were against us; they were tired of this foolish stuff of non-violence. When Dr. King started speaking, they started parading with banners that said, "Down with Non-Violence." When that was over, they herded Dr. King out of a back door, and he went back to Atlanta.

But I was there for two or three days after that, and I went into those meetings with the northern black leaders. At first they thought I was very foolish. "What you got that old woman for?" they said to Myles Horton.

But by the end of the conference they chose me to represent them in meetings with the other groups. They found out that I could present their ideas in a way that others could listen to. They were beginning to see how non-violence worked.

Just when the younger leaders were starting to understand non-violence, Dr. King was killed. That was in April, 1968. I was working in Charleston at the time. The shooting took place on a Thursday. The first thing I did was to take into my house a white minister and his family who had been working in a nearby town. They were afraid they would be hurt as black people expressed their anger.

Then I went around to the various islands and gathered groups to hold memorial services on Sunday. On Monday I got in a car and went to Atlanta for the big funeral on Tuesday. I didn't shed any tears—I was too busy. Not until I was back in Charleston did I feel the need to cry.

I look back at the period of the late fifties and sixties as being a watershed period in American history. We underwent a tremendous upheaval of change, and we did it with very little destruction. The movement itself was essentially non-violent. We consciously taught the message that we all lose when there is violence, and we can all win if we can find a way to resolve our differences without being destructive. I think the civil rights movement really demonstrated that.

The Role of Women

I WAS ON THE EXECUTIVE STAFF of SCLC, but the men on it didn't listen to me too well. They liked to send me into many places, because I could always make a path in to get people to listen to what I have to say. But those men didn't have any faith in women, none whatsoever. They just thought that women were sex symbols and had no contribution to make. That's why Rev. Abernathy would say continuously, "Why is Mrs. Clark on this staff?"

Dr. King would say, "Well, she has expanded our program. She has taken it into eleven deep south states." Rev. Abernathy'd come right back the next time and ask again.

I had a great feeling that Dr. King didn't think much of women either. He would laugh and say, "Ha, ha, ha. Mrs. Clark has expanded our program." That's all. But I don't think that he thought too much of me, because when I was in Europe with him, when he received the Nobel Peace Prize in 1964, the American Friends Service Committee people wanted me to speak. In a sort of casual way he would say, "Anything I can't answer, ask Mrs. Clark." But he didn't mean it, because I never did get the chance to do any speaking to the American Friends Service Committee in London or to any of the other groups.

When I heard the men asking Dr. King to lead marches in various places, I'd say to them, "You're there. You going to ask the leader to come everywhere? Can't you do the leading in these places?"

I sent a letter to Dr. King asking him not to lead all the marches himself, but instead to develop leaders who could lead their own marches. Dr. King read that letter before the staff. It just tickled them; they just laughed. I had talked to the secretaries before about it, and when the letter was read they wouldn't say a word, not one of them. I had a feeling that they thought Dr. King would have to do the leading. If you think that another man should lead, then you are looking down on Dr. King. This was the way it was.

Here was somebody from Albany, from Waycross, Georgia, from Memphis, Tennessee, from Chicago, from Detroit—all wanting him to come and lead a march. I felt that it wasn't necessary. I thought that you develop leaders as you go along, and as you develop these people let them show forth their development by leading. That was my feeling, but that was too much for them. They didn't feel as if that should be.

I think that there is something among the Kings that makes them feel that they are the kings, and so you don't have a right to speak. You can work behind the scenes all you want. That's all right. But don't come forth and try to lead. That's not the kind of thing they want.

When I went into that little town out from Macon and presented those people certificates of appreciation, Dr. King's secretary was terribly worried because he was hurt by it. He thought that I presented them and didn't call his name. But I did call his name. I said, "In the name of Dr. King and the SCLC we are glad to have you as affiliates of SCLC. We want to work with you in this town to get people registered to vote. First, they have to learn to read and write." He didn't know that I had said that, and he was blaming his secretary for letting me have the appreciation certificates to present to them.

But in those days I didn't criticize Dr. King, other than asking him not to lead all the marches. I adored him. I supported him in every way I could because I greatly respected his courage, his service to others, and his non-violence. The way I think about him now comes from my experience in the women's movement. But in those days, of course, in the black church men were always in charge. It was just the way things were.

Like other black ministers, Dr. King didn't think too much of the way women could contribute. But working in a movement he changed the lives of so many people that it was getting to the place where he would have to see that women are more than sex symbols. He always said that his wife should never leave home to do anything as long as they had small children. In 1965 I was in Pasadena, and Mrs. King was supposed to come out and give a concert because she was a great concert singer. She almost had to give up her career. She hasn't gotten back to it, either, because the men didn't feel as if it was right.

I see this as one of the weaknesses of the civil rights movement, the way the men looked at women. I think I know how the men got that way. I think about my mother, who had a feeling that black boys in the South could be conspired upon. She wanted to keep her boys right under her nose; she never wanted them away from her. She would always say: "A girl will bring you one trouble, but a boy can bring so many others. He can be arrested for stealing. He can be arrested for looking at a white." She'd name all these things that I think caused black mothers to feel as if black boys have to be very docile. Because they resented that, the black boys grew up feeling that women should not have a say in anything. That's what I think.

When I was working over on Johns Island, the women never could get up and give a suggestion. Esau Jenkins wouldn't listen to them, not at all. I remember one woman said, "Don't pay attention to that silly Esau. He ain't goin' to listen to ya." And that was the truth.

When Dr. King visited at Esau's house, Dr. King said, "Do you mean to tell me that you built this house and furnished it and that your wife didn't have any part of it?"

And do you know what Mrs. Jenkins said? She said, "If Esau like it, I like it."

That was the way most women were reared. My mother wasn't reared like that, though. No, she was the boss of her house.

I found all over the South that whatever the man said

had to be right. They had the whole say. The woman couldn't say a thing. Whatever the men said would be right, and the wives would have to accept it.

Out of these experiences I felt I wanted to be active in the women's liberation movement. Remember Virginia Durr, that friend of Rosa Parks in Montgomery? She also proved to be an excellent friend to me.

Virginia was with the National Organization of Women. When they had their first meeting in Washington, I think it must have been in 1958, she had me to come from Highlander to talk about the women of the South who failed to speak up when they knew what they wanted, about white women who would see their husbands doing wrong but dared not tell them, about black women who wouldn't speak at all because the husband had the right to say whatever.

Virginia Durr got me a room at a swell hotel, and I'd never had such a thing before in my life—a room that was all treated up to look like a wonderful place to live. I had a bedroom, a restroom, and also a sort of a little parlor on the side, but I really didn't get to use it very much. I was too busy in meetings, where we talked about the things that were happening in Alabama, the kind of segregation that those people were living under.

I was able to get a whole lot of things done through those women, because later on I went back there to talk to them about the kinds of things that women had to face in voter registration. For example, in Louisiana a black woman even had to say that she was not the father of an illegitimate child. South Carolina had in its law that a person registering had to swear that "I'm not guilty of arson or of wife-beating." One woman said, "How could I be a wife-beater, since I'm a woman?" Those were some of the things that came up in the liberation movement that I was able to talk to the women in Washington about.

I also went to Oak Ridge, Tennessee, to a meeting in May of '53 or '54. There were numbers of women at Oak Ridge whose husbands had come to work in that big atomic research plant there. I found out that those women were different. They would speak out. They were concerned about black and white women from various parts of the South who would never speak out.

These southern women were worried about their children; they wanted their children to do what they had a feeling for, but it was not possible because the husband had the real power over the whole family. Nothing that the women said could go. It had to be what the man said. One woman said that she as the wife could see the husband doing whatever he wanted to do with the women who worked on his farm, and still she could say nothing about it. She had to let it go just as she saw it. She could not do one thing.

That was quite a meeting at Oak Ridge. The wives of the workers at the atomic plant told their feelings, how they felt. They didn't see how the men should have all the say. They didn't see why women couldn't talk about the discrepancies that they noted. Anyway, I worked along with them.

There were many things that I felt we needed to change, but there were some points that I had different ideas about. I saw women in Maine and in the mountains of North Carolina driving tractors, and to me that was a terrible thing. I just didn't think that women had strength enough to do that type of thing. But there they were.

I still have a feeling that women weren't made to do the heavy lifting, and I think I got that from my father. He didn't like for us to lift a tub of water, didn't like to see a white woman with a bag of groceries in her arms. He would always say, "Hand it here, Missy; it's too heavy for you." I still have that feeling that there are things too heavy for a woman. I think that her backbone is not made for that kind of lifting.

Once I read an article which said that women are made differently, that the bone that goes from the end of their back up to the brain doesn't have the same kind of tissue or strength that the men have. Women shouldn't drink, the article said, because the alcohol would ruin that same bone and would lead to the brain; that's why women get drunk quicker than men and act real silly. I never will forget that article. I still think that there is a difference, that women become alcoholics quicker than men.

Now I do serve wine for Thanksgiving dinner and for Christmas dinner. That's a custom. We used to make eggnog and have a big bowl in the middle of the table, and the neighbors would come in celebrating Christmas and the New Year. Instead of the eggnog now we serve the wine. But I still don't care for alcoholic drinks at all. They make you foolish, make you real foolish.

But even though I think women are physically weaker than men and get drunk faster, I am all for women's liberation. This country was built up from women keeping their mouths shut. It took fifty years for women, black and white, to learn to speak up. I had to learn myself, so I know what a struggle it was.

I used to feel that women couldn't speak up, because when district meetings were being held at my home on Henrietta Street in Charleston, I didn't feel as if I could tell them what I had in my mind. Not at all. I thought it was up to the men to do that talking. Of course, my father always said that a woman needs to be quiet and just be in the home. I grew up with the idea that women didn't have a word to say. But later on, I found out that women had a lot to say, and what they had to say was really worthwhile. I changed my mind about women being quiet when they had something to say. I felt that surely the talk that the women had would be worthwhile, as well as what the men had to say. So we started talking, and have been talking quite a bit since that time.

As I look back into the early twenties, I see women both white and black who never dared to give a thought in any home or meeting. They were silent at all times. They did the chores and failed even to speak out about any wrong. In the late fifties and sixties in the United States there was a tremendous upheaval for women. They gained success and recognition. Before that, it was difficult for any woman in the U.S. to be recognized for her intellectual ability. For black women, the problem was two-fold: being a woman and being black.

Until recently black women have just been ignored in history books. Now books are coming out that show the impact that black women have had on the shaping of America. One example is *Black Women of Valor* by Olive Burt that tells about four black women—Juliette Derricotte, social worker; Maggie Mitchell Walker, banker; Ida Wells Barnett, journalist; and me—Septima Poinsette Clark, educator.

Many people think that the women's liberation movement came out of the civil rights movement, but the women's movement started quite a number of years before the civil rights movement. Virginia Durr asked me to come down and talk to the black women of the churches in Montgomery in 1955. I spoke at that church, and I was able to get a number of those women to come to Highlander.

The women of Montgomery played a major role in organizing the bus boycott, not just in carrying it out. Black women helped through their church groups, as well as through the Women's Political Council, started at Alabama State College. The women believed that if they supported protest, then the men would go along. But the men couldn't be out front leading—they had more to lose.

In the spring of 1957, a few months after we won the bus boycott in Montgomery, women organized a march on Washington, D.C. It was called "The Prayer Pilgrimage." That was six years before the big march of 200,000 people when Dr. King gave his "I Have a Dream" speech. The march in '57 was the largest civil rights demonstration ever staged by black Americans up to that time, and Mrs. Coretta King did the speaking.

In stories about the civil rights movement you hear mostly about the black ministers. But if you talk to the women who were there, you'll hear another story. I think the civil rights movement would never have taken off if some women hadn't started to speak up. A lot more are just getting to the place now where they can speak out.

PART II: THE BEGINNING
AND THE END

EDITOR'S NOTE:
*Septima Clark was born in 1898, thirty-five years after slavery
was abolished in the southern states. For the first twelve years after
the Civil War ended, federal troops occupied the South to try to
guarantee the freed slaves their civil and political equality. But in
1873 a depression began that within four years became the most
severe yet experienced in the United States. Farmers and workers
were beginning to rebel; the northern and southern elites re-approached
each other in order to protect themselves. This reconciliation between
northern and southern elites became clear in the Compromise of
1877, when the Republican party made concessions to the Democratic
party in order to win the disputed presidential race between Ruther-
ford Hayes and Samuel Tilden. As part of these concessions, the
Republicans agreed to remove from the South the Union troops,
who were one obstacle to the re-establishment of white supremacy.*

*For the twenty years after 1877 a fluid situation existed in he
South, during which different philosophies of race relations competed
for acceptance. Segregation, or the policy of setting black people
apart, had been used in the North prior to the Civil War, but it
was not introduced full-scale in the South until the end of the
nineteenth century.*

*During the 1890s the whole country suffered another severe
economic depression during which many people suffered dreadfully
from poverty, hunger, and insecurity. The U.S. government began
to fight colonial and racist wars to control the raw materials of the
Philippines, Cuba, and Puerto Rico. The Supreme Court held, in
a series of decisions, that segregation was compatible with the U.S.
Constitution, although earlier the Court had ruled segregation uncon-*

stitutional. The message went out that colored and black people were to be considered inferior. There had to be a scapegoat for the cruel disappointment of hopes suffered during the depression.

Between 1900 and 1920, the years of Septima Clark's coming of age, the South affirmed racism, and state after state enacted laws that legalized a full-scale system of segregation. These laws, which required blacks and whites to avoid contact as much as humanly possible, applied to all forms of public transportation, to sports and recreations, to employment, prisons, hospitals, schools, and ultimately to funeral homes, morgues, and cemeteries.

Racial intermarriage, or miscegenation as it was called, was forbidden as a contamination of the white race. But since love across racial lines had a long history in the United States, the laws against miscegenation had to contain a specific definition of who was black; they usually said that anyone who had one black ancestor out of eight must be considered black.

Septima as a child encountered a recently enacted social system. Her parents, relatives, and friends were just learning to deal with a segregated way of life. Septima's father had been born a slave and had gained his freedom when he was about seventeen; he was about fifty at Septima's birth. Her mother, never a slave, had been raised in Haiti under English law and custom; she was about thirty at Septima's birth. The two of them reacted to segregation in diametrically different ways.

Septima's Childhood

I HAVE TOLD ABOUT what it was like for me to work throughout the South helping people register and vote. Now I want to go much further back into the past and tell about what it was like to grow up under full segregation, how I learned to accept all the places I could not go, all the things I could not do. I want to tell about my parents and how they dealt with these issues and the qualities they passed on to me.

My father, Peter Porcher Poinsette, was born a slave on the Joel Poinsette Plantation. Joel Poinsette was a great botanist, and he brought a flowering tree from Mexico, when he was U.S. ambassador there. It is called the poinsettia today, and he was the one who introduced it into America.

They say Poinsette was a very good master, if you had to be on a plantation. His was called Casa Bianca, and it lay on the Wando River, about seventy miles from Charleston. Poinsette and his wife lived alone in this remote place, along with about sixty slaves who grew rice.

My father's mother was pregnant with him when she was brought from Africa. Joel Poinsette bought her in a slave market about 1846, and soon afterward my father was born. She had four more children—one real black girl, one white blue-eyed boy, and two brown boys. All of them worked as field hands on the plantation.

But my father, being the first of her children, got to live in the big house and take the children of his master to school every day. They rode on horseback, while he carried their books. There were two of them, and he would always carry their books into their classroom, come back out, put the horse up, and sit around under a tree regardless of the weather to wait until they were ready to go back home. Not once did he go inside to learn to read and write himself.

But my father never complained about the things in slavery. He talked about how the cook would sometimes put the key on the outside, and the slaves would come and get it so they could get some meat out of the smokehouse. If the master caught them, he would whip them. Father would tell us how they cried and ran around. But not once did he have a feeling that anything was wrong. He thought it was all right.

During the Civil War my father was old enough to carry wood and water to the soldiers. They were shooting the cannons against the Yankee ships in the harbor that came to free the slaves. My father was fighting on the side of his master. He believed in him.

Not until the end of the Civil War was my father actually free. He was about seventeen or eighteen then. He claimed that when they were free, they didn't like it too well. They thought they wouldn't have any food to eat anymore. There wasn't any work for them, and he said that numbers of them just cried.

After he was freed, my father went on a Clyde Line ship that used to go from the end of Florida up to New York. I really don't know what he did when he was working on that ship. I don't know whether he cooked or what.

After he left the Clyde Line, my father became a caterer. There used to be a little restaurant down on Tradd Street, and he sold food there. Then he catered for big parties; he went to white people's houses and served, especially for parties.

My father came out of slavery non-violent. He was a gentle, tolerant man who knew how to make the best of a situation.

My mother was something else. She was fiercely proud. She boasted that she was never a slave, but I have a feeling that somewhere down the line somebody paid her way out.

Born Victoria Warren Anderson, my mother had three distinct sets of brothers and sisters. The first set was mulatto, two girls with soft curly brown hair. Then came three ginger-colored boys with soft black hair. Then came three girls including my mother, Victoria. They were medium-brown with soft straight black hair. Their father was Indian, from the Muskhogean tribes who lived on the sea islands from Charleston to Savannah, Georgia.

My mother was born in Charleston but reared in Haiti. When she was very young, her mother died, and those three little girls were sent to Haiti to be raised by their older brothers, who were cigar makers there.

The English school teachers in Haiti did a very good job with my mother, because they taught her how to read and write. That made her the proud soul she was all her life.

When she was eighteen, her family moved to Jacksonville, Florida. There she met and married Peter Poinsette and moved with him to Charleston.

In 1905, when I was seven years old, my parents moved into a house on Henrietta Street. We didn't have any plumbing in that house, so we had to haul water in buckets. We had a fountain right at the front of our street there on that Marion Square, and that water was warm. We could go down there on Saturday night and get a bucket of that water, put it in a tub, and bathe.

A lady used to pay me 5¢ to bring twelve buckets of water for her from a well down to the corner so she could wash. My mother didn't want me to take that nickel. If people sent you to the store or to get water, she didn't want you to take money for it. She always said you must learn to share your services.

But sometimes we'd take that nickel, run into that store, buy that candy, and eat it before we carried the water home. Yes, Lord, I used to do the same thing with oil. When we'd have to go buy oil, I'd buy 2¢ worth of candy first, and then with what was left I'd get the oil and take it back home to fix the lamps.

Henrietta Street was really mixed, and it was just a one-block street. There was a Jewish family, a German one, and Irish and Italians. But the children didn't mix. The white children played in front of their door, and the black children played in front of their door. If we would skate by that Irishman's door, he would come out there and threaten to whip us. Nothing you could do about it. We couldn't skate by his door at all nor drive a goat-cart by his door.

I didn't worry about this. Somehow or other I didn't think about it then. No, we played right in the front where we were. We knew Mr. Berry. Sometimes we would sneak by his door, and he'd come out, and we'd run back. But it seemed like the parents never thought they could change the whole system, not at all. My mother would always say, "Just stay away from that man's door."

This is the real irony of the thing. We had two families on that street in which the mothers, who were black, and the fathers, who were white, were not married. One family was a woman with a German fellow, Kallenbeck, and she had two children for him. He would come and visit, and the man was fond of the woman. But they couldn't get married, because there was a law against blacks and whites marrying.

The funniest thing about it was my mother used to always say: "You can't go to the Kallenbeck's." Because the mother wasn't a married woman, the black people felt that you couldn't talk with them. I was about fourth or sixth grade when she got very sick. She wanted me to come and read the Bible to her, and my mother did let me go to do that.

Across the street was another fellow, a white man, who owned a strawberry farm. The woman with him had about eight children for him. But still we didn't play with them because the mother and father weren't married. "Being a kept woman," that is the way my mother used to say it. We went all the way uptown and played with our cousins instead of playing with the children on that street.

We walked uptown. We walked everywhere. No cars, not then. On Sunday afternoons sometimes, when my mother felt like it, she would take us to walk down King Street and back, from one end to the other. That was our recreation. That was the way we did it.

Sometimes she'd take us all the way to the Battery.

Everyone called it the Bott'ry. That was that wall down to the bottom of town. It was built before the Civil War to protect Charleston from Yankee ships. When I was a child there was a beautiful park along the wall. Blacks weren't allowed to sit on the benches in that park, except on the Fourth of July, which the old-time whites considered a Yankee holiday. But we could walk along there and feel the cool breezes from the ocean.

The Battery was about two miles from our house on Henrietta Street. First we had to pass Marion Square, with its fountain of warm water and a military school for the wealthy white boys. Then we came to Broad Street. Below that was the area where the rich white people lived in mansions cooled by sea breezes. My father's restaurant was on Tradd Street, just below Broad Street by one block. That was considered a grand outing, when my mother walked us children to the Battery.

There were eight children in my family—four girls and four boys. There was one girl older than me. I was the second child. My brother, Peter, is next to me. Then there was a sister. She's dead now, and her son lives in New York. Another brother, and he died. Then another brother, there were two. Then came my sister, Lorene, nearly fifteen years between us. Then my baby brother, who is in Mt. Vernon, New York.

Septima is the Latin word for seventh, and in Haiti it means sufficient. My parents named me Septima, and I wondered why, because I was not the seventh child and neither was I sufficient, because six came after me. But I got that name for an aunt down in Haiti whose name was Septima Peace, Sufficient Peace; I was named for her. I was supposed to be sufficient peace, but I certainly wasn't sufficient, and I don't know about the peace, because I did so many things that wasn't peaceful. I'm just getting to the place where I can have peaceful ideas now.

My mother was the disciplinarian person in that family. She had a wonderful plan, I feel. She had a schedule for every child and for every day of the week. She had to wash and iron

Septima Clark (right) with her sister, Lucille, and her brother, Peter, in 1924.

to help with the income. But she did it, and she taught us to do that kind of work also. Every day we had special chores. In the morning when I cooked the breakfast my sister had to take care of the little ones—get them dressed for school. When she cooked, then I had to do the dressing of the smaller children. My brother, who was younger than I, had to sweep down the steps and cut paper for the outdoor toilet. That was his work, and then rake the yard sometimes.

Each of the older children always had a younger child as our ward to see that that child was fed, had clean clothes, didn't have holes in his clothes or anything of that type. If he had, then the older one got the whipping. That's the way my mother did it. I know if Lorene had a hole in her underpants, I'd get the whipping. I was expected to mend the hole.

We could only play on Friday afternoons. We always had work to do all during the week when we came home from school. Friday afternoons we could go to my aunt's house and play with her children. If we ate at our cousin's house one weekend, we couldn't eat the next weekend. We'd have to wait until two weeks around before we could eat again. That was mother's way. She said that you don't want them to think that you're so hungry for food that you have to eat every time you go to the house.

On Sundays we could not play at all. We went to two Sunday Schools, one in the morning and one in the afternoon. When we came back in the afternoon we sat on the porch, and they served us some peanuts and candy, and we could sing around an organ that we had. My sister could play the organ, but we never could go out in the yard and play ball, because that was against the religion to do anything like that on Sunday. Of course, we didn't have radio or television then, so the only thing you could do was sing, or go walking, and then go to bed.

During the week one hour in the early evening, say from six to seven o'clock, we had to put time on our lessons. Mother took time out from her work and helped you with the lessons. You'd better learn to read that geography or get those answers. You'd have to do it during that one hour, then you went to bed. I used to really dislike being put to bed early. My older sister could stay up a little longer, and I wanted to, too. But I couldn't; I had to go to bed.

My mother ironed, and she had a great big chimley upstairs in her bedroom. She had a big fire with the irons in front of it to heat. We slept on a bed right across the front of the fire and never bothered. Hot? Yes, it was hot, but you didn't say anything about it. You went to your bed and slept, and she ironed until way late in the night.

One time when my mother was talking to a sister of hers, I tried to correct her, to tell her that she wasn't saying the thing just right. It didn't happen that way. She slapped me in the mouth and knocked out a tooth, and she made me wash out my mouth with salt water and get right up and go about my business. That night, because she had done that, I didn't want to say my prayers and say, "God bless mama." So she whipped me again; I had to get a real good whipping. I still wouldn't say that "God bless mama," so she just threw me over the bed.

To whip us, my mother used a strap like a belt, but it didn't have buckles on it. Now she wouldn't whip you on Sundays. If you did anything wrong on Sundays, like we would take her ham and cut a piece off when she went to church or suck the milk out of the can, when she came back she wouldn't whip you on Sunday. But she'd whip you early Monday morning.

At the time, I felt angry about the whippings. Every time I got a whipping I felt angry about it. Some children will laugh. My brother used to laugh, but I didn't. My sister used to run, but I wouldn't run from a whipping. I'd stand there and take mine, although I was angry. My mother would beat my sister good when she caught her; she didn't like you to run from her.

But now I'm very happy when I think of what my mother did. I'm glad for the schedule that she had, the way she made us work, and the way she made us do things around the house. I think it was very good for us all.

Now my father didn't like to whip. When my mother would report a child, he didn't say anything or she'd give him a slap. But he still didn't say anything. When she went to meetings, we would be sitting down talking about how harsh she was with her treatment, and he would say to us: "Whatever she does, she's doing it for your own good." He never talked against her; she was the person who was right.

Because my father was not educated, he wanted his children to learn to read and write. The one thing he would whip you for, if he ever whipped you, was for not wanting to go to school. I can remember when a teacher whipped me for not being able to spell the word "name." I didn't want to go to school the next morning, but he made me go. He went along with me and carried my bookbag. I was angry the whole time, but I had to go.

Those were the days. I really enjoyed those days. We had a good time, unless I got a whipping. Then I was angry. But other than that, I was happy most of the time, really happy.

One thing I appreciated about my parents. We had breakfast before we went to school. My mother tied up a lunch and gave it to you to take. She also gave you a penny if you wanted to buy a piece of granut cake with peanuts in it or molasses cake with coconut in it. When you came from school, you had a dinner, and around 7 o'clock at night you had a supper. In the wintertime you had three hot meals, and in the summertime you had two hot meals and a cold supper at night. We used to go across that green at Marion Square and buy six loaves of bread. They were two for only a nickel. That was the supper bread. Every Sunday morning we had fish and grits and tomato sauce. She'd be sure to see that you had a good breakfast before you went out there to Sunday School, and she taught me to cook early. I got to the place where I could fix a real good meal, get it done.

We bought most of our food. We used to plant okra and corn, sometimes tomatoes and string beans, that's all. The rest we got from men who came around with pushcarts. They sold shrimp for 10¢ a plate, fish for 25¢ a string. The milk came in little cans; you could buy 5¢ or 10¢ or 15¢ worth of milk. Each child would have a small cup of milk with grits for breakfast.

My father was the best cook, I felt, better than my mother, but I'd better not have said that before her. He could cook the greens and pig feet and things she never bothered with.

I learned from my mother not to be afraid. She was a very courageous person, and I could see her in action doing many things there on Henrietta Street. She had a way of letting you know that she was never afraid of anyone, and she wanted you to be able to stand your ground regardless of where you were or whatever happened.

For example, a man did something on a street back of us, and he jumped the fence and came into our yard. My brother had a goat. They always had little goat wagons for the children at that time. This man got behind the goat under the house, and when the policeman came to hunt the man, he couldn't find him. The dog would head the policeman off from the goat, and the man was behind the goat, so the policeman could never get the man out.

My mother said, "What you doing in my yard? Who told you you could come in here? You're not supposed to come into my yard."

The policeman replied that he was pursuing a criminal.

She said, "I'm a little piece of leather, but I'm well put together, so don't you come in here."

My mother did many things like this. I appreciate them because I really feel that it helped me to be able to stand in front of the Klansmen and the White Citizens' Councils, of large groups that were hostile. I never felt afraid, and I think it was due to the fact that my mother showed so much courage back in those early days. I felt that if she could do it way back then, then I could.

My mother was very active in her church, Bethel Methodist. The money she got from her washing and ironing she used to keep up her church dues. She wasn't going to let the church go lacking. If she needed a piece of ice (we didn't have frigidaires at that time), and she had money for insurance or money for the church, she would rather drink the water hot. That's going to be for the church, that for the insurance. She kept it just like that.

I've never been able to do that. I spend whatever I have for where it's needed. I do get my bills paid, but I wouldn't drink no hot water and save the money if I knew I needed a piece of ice. She'd do it every time. Her church was really something to her. She had to walk down there every time she'd go. She never got too old to walk.

I was christened in my mother's church, but I went to the church where my brother works one Good Friday. They were having a week of revival down there that night, and I felt a difference. I was thirteen years of age, and so I became born again, as I say, at the age of thirteen. Then I had to go for several months and be trained up into the workings of my church. After that I was confirmed on an Easter Sunday in my church.

I've been working in the church all my life. In the Sunday School when I got big enough I became chairman of the youth group. A little bit later on our church bought an organ. The lady who was chairman took sick, and raising money for that organ fell on me. I went from house to house raising over $4000. That was when I was eighteen years of age.

Now my father was a little different. He was a member of the church but went very seldom. Most of the time he was working on Sundays. He never was anybody like a leader, nothing like that. He wasn't a man for organizations.

But he was respected in the community. People knew my father because he catered parties, because he had that little restaurant down on Tradd Street, and because he was a former slave of Joel Poinsette. The Cheves family was related to Joel Poinsette. They remembered my father all through his life, and he would go to visit them quite a number of times. They were particularly fond of him.

There were three things I felt I learned from my father. One was that he wanted you to always be truthful. Next, he wanted you not to exalt yourself, but to look at the culture of others and see whether or not you could strengthen their weaknesses and try to investigate how you could improve yourself towards them. Then, too, he talked about having Christ in your life. This is one thing that helps you to understand people better. If you can get the spirit of Christ into your life, you will learn to see others as Christ saw them and be able to live with them and help them to live with themselves. I feel that sitting around that pot–bellied stove he really gave us three very good things to look forward to—being truthful, strengthening people's weaknesses, and seeing that there is something fine and noble in everybody.

Now let me tell you about my schooling. My parents were determined that I would get a good education. First I went to public school. We had about a hundred first-grade children on what we called the ABC gallery. They had outside toilets, and all we had time to do was to go back and forth to the toilets. The principal would come around to see if anybody had been bad and give you a whipping, and then it was time to get ready to go home again. That gallery was built just like bleachers for people today, and if you fell asleep while you were sitting up there, the teacher would have you whipped. The teacher had about one hundred children. It was something to think about.

Later on my mother took me away from that school and sent me to a private school. There were lots of black women who had little schools in their homes—in their kitchens, in their dining rooms, or in little shed rooms. We went to one of those, and I really learned in that kind of a school.

The school I went to was in the back room of a two-room home. There were about forty children and two teachers, an older woman and her niece. The older woman taught the bigger pupils, and the niece taught the younger ones. Most of these Charleston black women who taught private school had gone to the public schools in the days following the ending of the Civil War. The woman who conducted the school I attended had gone to one of these early public schools, but the younger one had graduated from a private school in Charleston, Avery Institute.

I went to that woman's home for three years. Tuition was usually $1 a month. I greatly admired the woman who operated our school. She had great pride and demanded that her pupils have pride, too. In the first place, the children of her school were a select group. She didn't take just anybody who had the money for tuition. She chose her pupils from the blacks who boasted of being free issues, people who had never been slaves. These people constituted a sort of upper caste.

Our teacher required that we act in a manner befitting our superior position. Her rules would seem strange today. Chewing gum was strictly forbidden. If you went into the schoolroom late or should happen to laugh at something taking place, you might expect a whipping. If you missed a spelling word, she would bring you up to the front of the room and whip each letter into the palm of your hand. Pity the poor child who missed "Constantinople." But I remember her as a great teacher.

When I got to the fourth grade I went back to the public school, where I was able to get a very good type of education. But there was one thing—no black teachers were teaching in the city of Charleston at that time. Segregation was at its height, and all of the children who went to the ABC gallery and the Mars Street School were black. But they were taught by white teachers. Black teachers could not teach black children in public schools. White teachers taught both black and white students, but they taught them in separate buildings— Mary Street School for the whites and Mars Street School for the blacks.

We had white teachers who were trained at Memminger Normal School. They didn't like for black children to speak to them in the streets; I guess they didn't want other people to know they were teaching blacks. They were embarrassed to be teaching black children, and they would have you whipped.

That was one of the things we had to work against. When I finished high school and had a teaching certificate and went to teach, the first thing I worked on was to get black teachers in the public schools in Charleston, because I felt that it was such a disgrace to have children whipped just because they said, "How you do, Miss Gibbs?" or whoever the teacher was.

I have wanted to be a teacher since very early, and let me tell you how that happened. My mother was renting all the time. My parents didn't own their home, and she was renting from a man who owned a grits mill. He lived right in back of us on another street, and he'd come through an alley way and knock on our door to collect his rent. It was $5 a week that she had to pay for that house. One day she didn't have the money to pay him and, boy, he serenaded her. I heard him, and I felt, "If I could be a teacher, I could have this money, and my mother wouldn't have this kind of humiliation." Right from that time I have wanted to be a teacher, and I must have been either nine or ten years old then.

I loved children so much in the early days on my street that I would gather them and take them to a parade or for some recreation or to Sunday School on Sunday mornings. The people in the neighborhood called me "Little Ma." They really meant "Little Mother," for I was considered a little mother to all these children and would pick them up and take them with me, and the parents were glad for me to do that, because it gave them a chance to get away from their own children.

Once when I was going to the public school, a boy yelled out the window, "Le Ma." They didn't say "little"; they said "le." I didn't answer him. I was ashamed of the name then. From that time on I wouldn't answer people when they called me "Le Ma." I disliked a nickname; I didn't want them to know I had one. But I really had one.

A high school for blacks didn't come in Charleston until 1912. That's when we got our first high school. It was such an event that President Taft came down to the dedication of the first building of this high school, Burke Vocational Institute. I can remember we stood out in the street and listened to him. One girl in my class presented him with a bouquet of flowers. We thought it was such a strange thing—he picked her up and kissed her, a little black girl. We didn't think that that could ever be possible.

Burke Institute was what you'd call a middle school today. It was just sixth, seventh, and eighth grades. It didn't get to the ninth until later on. I didn't know it then, but the state of South Carolina spent only 11 percent of its school funds on educating black children, even though there were more of us than there were of white children.

I went to Burke Vocational Institute for one year, and then I took an examination to go to Avery Normal Institute, a private school for educating black teachers. When I went to Avery from the sixth grade at Burke, I was able to go into the ninth grade.

Avery was not a new school. It had been around since the Civil War ended in 1865. A white church group in Philadelphia, the American Missionary Association, organized it to teach former slaves who had been freed.

The man who set up the school was named Francis Louis Cardozo. His portrait hung in the front hall of the school, and I was always very proud of him. He was born in Charleston. His father was the Jewish editor of a newspaper, and his mother was half black and half Indian. They couldn't marry, but they sent their son to Europe to be educated. He became the first black secretary of state in South Carolina under the new government elected after the Civil War when blacks could vote.

In the tenth grade at Avery Institute I took an examination to teach, and I passed. But my mother didn't want me to stop school until I had finished the twelfth grade. That would give me what they called the Licentiate of Instruction, which was similar to two years of college. So I went back and took two more years, and in 1916 I finished Avery Normal Institute.

Before I graduated, Avery got a new principal, the first black one since Francis Cardozo. A few black teachers taught at Avery, and they lived in the same dormitory with the white teachers from New England. The white men who governed Charleston had never been very happy about this arrangement, or even about the existence of the school. So when a black man became principal, it was too much for them. They ruled that black and white teachers could not live in the same dormitory.

This brought a lot of sorrow because the school had to get rid of its white teachers. Two of the most beloved teachers —Miss Marsh and Miss Tuttle—were white. They were permitted to stay an extra two years, my last two years, too.

When I was a senior at Avery, I took another teacher's examination and passed. If I could find a job, I would be set to begin my career of teaching. But just before the school year ended, the two white teachers and the principal came to visit my parents. "Septima is college material," they said. "We are hoping she can find some way to go to Fisk University in Tennessee."

Father and mother were both most anxious for me to go to college, but how could they arrange such a thing? The cost, they found, would be $19 a month. But $19 in those days was a tremendous amount. The cost of sending me to Avery had been but $1.50 a month, and that had been hard to come by. My mother, by working day and night, couldn't add enough to my father's earnings to send me away to college and take care of the other children. I knew it, even though she felt after the visit of the principal and the two white teachers that she would have to send me.

I argued against their trying to send me to Fisk. Had the situation been different, I would have loved to go. But I wasn't willing for them to attempt it.

Teaching, Marriage
and Children

TO BECOME THE WOMAN I was in 1956, I had to develop from the girl I was in 1916. Since I couldn't go to college, I had to learn in other ways. From my high school graduation until I became director of education at Highlander, I spent forty years growing up.

You know, the measure of a person is how much they develop in their life. Some people slow down in their growth after they become adults. You can hardly tell they are changing at all. But you never know when a person's going to leap forward, or change around completely. Just think of how much Martin Luther King, Jr., grew in his life. That was the greatest thing about him. Or think of Esau Jenkins. Or of Bernice Robinson.

I've seen growth like most people don't think is possible. I can even work with my enemies because I know from experience that they might have a change of heart any minute.

Sometimes my own growth embarrasses me. I don't like to admit, even to myself, that I was once ill at ease with white people or so middle-class in my attitudes that I had a hard time teaching poor people. But I overcame those things, and I'll tell you how it took forty years.

Since I wasn't going to college, I had to find a job teaching. The public schools of Charleston still did not hire black teachers, so I wouldn't be able to get a job and live at home. The South Carolina law said that blacks could teach on the islands surrounding, or in the surrounding communities, but never in the city of Charleston.

When I was a senior at Avery Institute, we had a minister at the Methodist United Church who looked out for his senior students. When I was coming out in 1916, he told me about some trustees who wanted a teacher over on Johns Island.

After seeing those trustees, I was able to get a job way down to the southern end of Johns Island. It was called Promise Land, and it was Promise Land School. It was a two-teacher school, and it had two rooms. One hundred and thirty-two children were down there because there were big farming plantations down at Promise Land. The school was made of logs, and it had clay in between to keep the wind from coming in during the wintertime. It had shutters, but no window panes, no glass, no window sashes at all. Whenever the wind was blowing on one side, you had to keep those shutters closed. You opened up the other side so you could have some light. There was a big chimley in the middle, and the girls would get grass to sweep the floor with. We had no kind of thing for housekeeping. The boys cut wood and brought it in so you could heat in the wintertime.

There were two of us teachers. I was a teaching principal. At first, both of us got $25 a month for teaching over there, and a little later on in the year they increased my pay to $35 a month. The other teacher had the first through the third grade, and I had the fourth through the eighth. Our school was creosoted black. A lot of people said the school was black to show that black children were in there.

There were three white children down to the end of that island, and they had a little school across the road from our school. It was a one-room school, white-washed white on the outside. There they had a bucket and a dipper. That teacher had a little bit more equipment in her school than we had in ours, although we had those 132 children, and she had only three.

The white teacher was earning $85 a month for three children, while the two of us got $60 for 132 children. Wasn't that something? But you know I did a lot with my $35. I used to send my check home. My mother cashed it, and she sent me back $10. I paid $8 a month board, and then I'd take my $2 to buy chicken or turkey and send it back on that boat to my mother. Then, too, I was able to carry a 5¢ savings club at the bank. With that, I bought a bicycle for my brother Peter for Christmas and a little bit of cloth for Lorene to have a dress that she could sling around in.

The children who came to school had to walk in the mud for many miles or paddle across the creeks. They were happy to get out of working in the fields, so they weren't worried. The big children didn't come in until after the harvest, around the later part of November. Most of the time they had to bring their little sisters or brothers—the three-year-olds and the four-year-olds. We had benches without backs, and they knelt on the floor to do their writing and put the pages on the top of the bench that they were supposed to be sitting on. When it was very cold and we had the fire, the children in the front got the heat. The ones in the back stayed cold all day.

So did the teacher. My feet got swollen and red. It was very cold the first winter that I spent over there, and my feet were not accustomed to that extreme cold. Therefore, I had what they call chilblains, which is really frostbite. I had frostbitten feet, which were very uncomfortable for a long time. No doctors being on the island, I did what the people told me to do. That was to roast white potatoes and put your heel in that potato, which made the thing worse.

Finally I had to come to the city and get something done by a doctor. The doctor in Charleston anointed my feet with some kind of ointment that took the swelling away, and the fever came out of the heels and toes. I was afraid I was going to lose my toes there for a while, but they finally got all right. That happened in December, and in January I was right back on the island. The only thing I did, though, I bound my feet with a towel when I had to walk through the deep mud going to school and coming back, which kept them warm.

I must say the children were well-behaved. We really didn't have any discipline problems. The parents were sure that they could behave themselves in school, and if you told the parents about them doing anything, the parents would do the whipping.

We had no blackboards at the time that I went over. Finally, we got a blackboard and a piece of round chalk. But most of the time we would bring from the city a dry cleaner's bag and write on that bag things they could copy. For reading we had to make up stories about the things around them—the trees, the foliage, the animals. They learned to read those words first.

We used quite a few African words, because on Johns Island we had quite a few Africans who had come by way of the Bahamas to South Carolina on that ship, "Wanderer," the last ship that carried Africans to be sold into slavery. So numbers of those words were part of them, and we could use those words to teach.

They used "goober" for peanut and "cooter" for turtle, probably from the Timbuktu word "kuta." They used "terrogate" most of the time in speaking about people or things that harassed or scared them.

The language spoken on Johns Island was exactly the same as that of the early blacks, who had just come from Africa. They created their own language, called Gullah, by mixing French, German, and English with the different African languages they brought. Since many African languages don't use that "th" sound, the early blacks said "th" as "d." I wasn't over there any length of time before I was saying "dischere" and "dat" myself.

When I taught reading, I put down "de" for "the," because that's the way they said "the." Then I told them, "Now when you look in a book, you're going to see "the." You say "de," but in the book it's printed "the."

Anyway, to teach reading I wrote their stories on the dry cleaner's bags, stories of their country right around them, where they walked to come to school, the things that grew around them, what they could see in the skies. They told them to me, and I wrote them on dry cleaner's bags and tacked them on the wall. From the fourth grade through the sixth grade they all did that same reading. But they needed that because it wasn't any use to do graded reading when they had not had any basic words at all.

After they learned the stories about their own island, I was able to get some books through the county system. I call it vicarious experiences—books that give stories of the midwest and the west. They had never heard about a seal, so we had to find books that could tell them about things like that, or stories of the great corn fields in the midwest where farmers made thousands of dollars. I was never able to get enough books so that each child could have one. But as I told those stories, they listened. One thing about people who can't read, they have good memories, and they can give you back the stories you tell them. That's what you put down for them to read.

That's the way I taught all the time. It's a task that teachers have to learn to do. You can't say. "Get a book and open it." You have to do all of that introduction. You have to say, "Look at this picture. Does it look like people are living here?" If it's a house with smoke coming out of the chimley, then they know that some people are living there or smoke wouldn't be coming out of the chimley. This is the way you build up your story; that's the way I do.

I think the young teachers today, because they have so much material, rely so much on the material that they don't use their own creative ability. Your creative ability is the thing that you need to pull out of these children their creative ability, make their eyes see what is in that picture.

It's surprising that I had so many children who became very competent. Some of them came to Charleston and made excellent teachers. One was the first black fellow who worked at the Navy Yard in engineering. Then Harold Stevens from Kaiwah Island, who had to paddle over to our school every morning because there was no bridge whatsoever, he is now one of the highest-paid lawyers in the country. He lives in New York. The young woman who presides in my church was one of my seventh grade students. Year before last she had three small churches in Massachusetts, but she'd rather come home. Now she's working with my minister and teaching during the day at one of the schools.

Living on Johns Island was quite a struggle for me. My mother came to visit once, and she was shocked at the crude conditions. But she didn't want me to quit.

To get to Johns Island we had to take a little gasoline launch and ride nine hours, going through the creeks. There were no bridges at that time. Bridges weren't built until 1945, not until then. All that time we had to go in the gasoline launches. Coming back, people would bring their hogs, and the hogs would be in there with all their manure. You'd be sitting right up there with them. You had to; that's the only way you could get back home. We stayed on the island most of the time from September to Christmas and then from Christmas to June.

When I landed, I was taken ten miles by horse and buggy to the Bishop family, where I boarded. The Bishops were black. They owned their own farm and had one of the bigger houses on the island. Mr. Bishop built it himself out of green lumber. When those boards dried, they shrank and left lots of cracks for the wind to blow through.

I had an attic room when I first went there to stay, and there was a lantern up in the ceiling to see by. There was one big chimley downstairs on the first floor. When everybody went to bed on Saturdays, I'd get my bath in front of that chimley. Water was very scarce, so when I'd get through bathing myself, then I would wash out my underwear in that same pan of water. During the week they had a tin basin on the back porch, and this is what you washed your face in in the morning.

The water came from surface wells. That's one reason why so many people got sick, because there were no toilets. They went outside and used the bushes, and when it rained all that water drained into the surface wells. That water was really impure.

The lady with whom I stayed didn't feel it was wise to buy pots. If she had a tomato can, she cooked most of the time in that. They had some kind of a frying pan because they got a lot of food from the sea, and they fried the fish in the frying pan. Sometimes they would let the ashes in the chimley burn down and get real hot and put the fish with scales on it in those ashes. Then when the fish got hot, they would scale it off, and that would be your breakfast—fish, plus grits.

But one thing I found over there in 1916. They grew vegetables but sent them away and didn't eat them themselves. They didn't eat their greens. They would ship them. Because of that, there was a real epidemic of pellagra. They ate mostly fatback and grits, but that food didn't have enough niacin, or vitamin B3, in it. So numbers of them suffered with pellagra and had the color come out of their lips. When it got to their hands, they were in bad shape. Numbers of them died from the scourge of pellagra. Scientists didn't figure out until about twenty years after I left the island that pellagra was caused by lack of niacin.

Newspapers were scarce things on Johns Island. People used to come to the city and buy them in bundles because they papered their house with them. Even the white planters did that. You could look in their living room and see all the Katzenjammer kids on the wall. They made a paste out of flour and water, boiled it, and put up those newspapers. And if a place leaked, why, you'd see it all coming down.

It was real fun for me over there. I never had a chance to walk over as much land as I did while I was there. On Saturdays I walked sometimes five miles and back, because there were ten black schools scattered over the island. It was full of plantations, and there were lots of children, so these one-teacher schools were scattered around. Then, too, the people had little plots of land that they worked themselves. In the afternoons, when I came from school, it was fun for me to help them drop seed in their garden, when they were planting corn or okra or cabbage. I really enjoyed it.

Nearly everyone around Johns Island spoke of me as being "Miss Seppie." It was hard for them to say "Septima," and that Poinsette was pretty hard, too. They used to say, "Setila" and all different kinds of things. So instead they said,

"Miss Seppie." All over the island I was known as "Miss Seppie."

There were very few people over there who could read. They wanted to speak in church or at a large meeting, and they did not know how to read at all. So for my own pleasure at nights I would teach the adults how to read and to write. It was really a kind of recreation for me to work with them at nights after they got out of the field.

In the summertime when I came home to Charleston, I always found some work to do. I'd get up at 6 o'clock in the morning, and I'd be going down to Miz Gordon's boarding house. I wouldn't get away from there until 9 o'clock at night. I'd serve three meals a day, and in between I'd wash the table napkins and iron them. She paid us $9 a week. That was big money. I worked Sunday, every day. But working was the thing that never worried me. I was brought up working, so I can always work.

I stayed there on Johns Island from 1916 to 1919, and then Avery Institute wanted me to teach. Avery's black principal wanted to expand the fifth and sixth grades. He came to my house and offered me $30 a month. I took that job teaching sixth grade and stayed in the city that year.

That was the year that an artist here, who was president of the NAACP, decided that we needed to do something about getting black teachers in the public schools of Charleston. We had to go to bat against that law.

When we first went to the legislators and asked for black teachers in Charleston, they said that only the mulattoes wanted that. So I took my class and went from door to door and got signatures of parents who wanted black teachers in the public schools. We got wives of the draymen and the domestic workers to sign slips. I got 20,000 signatures, not by myself, but with others helping. Those signatures convinced the legislature. In 1920 we got black teachers in Charleston, and in 1921 we got black principals.

It's the funniest thing with me. I never had any romances in high school. I guess when you haven't had association, when you just work and go to school and come home and be with your parents—that's the most dangerous situation. You need to have wider experience. This is what I think.

When I was teaching I fell in love with this guy from the Navy named Nerie Clark. My mother thought it was terribly strange. She said, "Somebody must have put some voodoo on you, cause you never bothered about boys. How did this happen?"

I met this sailor in Charleston. World War I was just over, and ships were streaming in from Europe, bringing home the soldiers. I was serving as a hostess at an open house for servicemen, and that's how I met Nerie Clark. His ship left the next day, and I just really didn't think I'd ever see him again.

Four months later, in the spring, Nerie's ship put in at Norfolk, Virginia. He used his three-day pass to visit me, but I was in the middle of graduation activities and hardly had a minute for him. But I walked him to his train and kissed him so hard that the blue dye rubbed off his uniform on my white shirtwaist.

In my little time with this sailor I had learned that he was eight and a half years older than I was. He had grown up in Hickory, North Carolina, in the mountains. Sixth grade was as far as they had schools for blacks there. He worked in the Navy as a cook. He was hardworking and liked fashionable clothes. He was also several shades darker than me, which my caste-conscious mother noticed right away.

In the fall of 1920 I went up to teach in McClellanville, a sleepy fishing village thirty-five miles north of Charleston. I took that job because I could earn $60 a month there.

In the early spring I had a proposal of marriage from a minister there. I refused him. I felt I would not be able to meet the requirements of a minister's wife. My behavior would be on display, and I was afraid that I would fail.

Nerie Clark's ship returned to Charleston later on that spring. Somehow or other he found me. He came up with the mailman. We talked again, and he decided that he wanted to marry me. Somehow or other we both got that same notion.

Of course, I didn't feel as if I could marry without my mother's consent. So he came back to Charleston to buy a ring and get my mother's consent, which she did not give. She said, "You're marrying somebody you don't know," which was pretty true, "and you marry him over my dead body," or something to that effect.

Since I had never fallen in love before, I had a feeling that this was my chance. This was my life, so I went ahead with it.

I got married at the home of the people where I was boarding. We had a supper that night after the marrying. He had to get back on his ship and go to Rotterdam, Holland.

Septima Clark in 1928.

Then I had a baby girl. I called her Victoria for my mother, but she didn't live but twenty-three days. I felt sure that it was my sin that caused that. I had disobeyed my mother, and I thought that's why this baby didn't live. I went down on the Battery, and I thought so much about drowning myself. My mother must have thought about it, too, because she sent my brother on a bicycle to look for me. He found me sitting down there. I changed my mind, I guess, and came home.

That baby was born without a rectum. I didn't know what happened. It wasn't born in the hospital. It was born at home with a midwife, and the midwife hadn't noticed that the baby didn't have a rectum and that the stools were coming through the vagina, until it got very sick and had a fever. They took it to the hospital and operated on it, but it died.

My husband had gone to sea at that time. That's what made me feel so terrible about it. We buried that baby, and when he came back I had to tell him about it, which was sad. There was nothing else I could do. Right after that we left and went to North Carolina to his people, and I got pregnant again.

When my husband came out of the Navy, we went to Dayton, Ohio. This baby was born in a hospital in Dayton—a healthy boy that we named Nerie for his father.

My happiness didn't last long. While I was still in the hospital in Dayton, I learned that my husband had been divorced from one woman and was virtually living with another one right there in Dayton. He asked me to leave Dayton as soon as I could.

I went back to my husband's parents in Hickory, North Carolina. Ten months later I got a phone call from Dayton—my husband was on his deathbed with bad kidneys.

I got back in time to say good-bye to my deeply ashamed husband. I took his body home for burial and pieced together all the sweet notes he had written me, so the minister could help the family feel good. The casket lay in his mother's living room, and his ten-month old son, just learning to walk, swung on the handles as if it were a toy.

The girlfriend in Dayton sent a spray of roses, which my brother-in-law put in a garbage can. I would not have done that. I would not allow hate to enter my heart. I felt sorry for my husband rather than anger. I pitied any person who could not keep his vows.

I never felt as if I wanted to marry again. I had a feeling that no man could treat this other man's child right. Funny things happen. I couldn't stand nobody talking about my son.

My son stayed with his grandmother in the hills of North Carolina most of the time after that. It caused me a lot of sorrow to decide to leave my son with his grandparents. I hated it so much. But I had to go teach, and I used to cry every time. When I went to summer school, pulling up my credits, it was hard for me to leave him.

He finished high school at sixteen and went down to Greensboro to go to college. After two years there they took him out for the Army. That was the hardest thing in my life. I said if he just had a father alive then, we could share this. I had to go to the bus stop with him as he was going to boot camp up in Chicago, Illinois. When they were putting that flag up on Iwo Jima Hill, I just knew he was going to be killed. I couldn't sleep that night. But I can usually work under stress. I did a whole thesis for my master's degree while he was in the Army.

My son had six children. The last one was born with a damaged brain. This little handicapped boy stayed with me until he was twelve, so I say that my son's grandmother kept him, and I had his little boy.

After my husband died I taught for a year in the mountains near his family. But I felt that I had been torn away from my friends of the Low Country, of my beloved Charleston. When my baby was two-and-a-half years old, I returned to Johns Island and began teaching again at that same Promise Land School.

After three more years I decided to move to Columbia, South Carolina. I hated to give up my work on Johns Island, but I was a widow with a young son, and I knew I must look ahead. I had been attending summer school in Columbia during the vacation months, and I knew that salaries for teachers there were about $65 a month.

My teaching in Columbia opened my eyes in many ways. There I first participated in interracial meetings. Whenever speakers came to the colleges in Columbia, black people were invited. Of course, we were segregated by race; we blacks sat in a section designated for us. But we could see and hear. I also joined many clubs and civic groups, such as the Federated Women's Club, a White Christmas Dance, and an annual play to raise money. This work proved to be good training for me in dealing with audiences and organizing programs of all kinds.

During those years at Columbia I went to summer school and took extension courses. As far back as the summer of 1930, in fact, I went to Columbia University in New York City. I decided to go there because I felt I wasn't getting the results from teaching in Columbia, South Carolina, that I should have gotten from those children. We had children of professors and doctors, and still they couldn't read according to what the manuals said they should. They could never pull themselves up to read 135 words a minute. I did tests all the time. I would watch the watch and give them a paragraph to read, and I found that they could never get higher than 93 words a minute. I said something must be wrong in the teaching, and I had to find out what it was.

I went to Columbia University then, and I took a course in math and one in curriculum building for exceptionally dull children. There I found out how to use the expressions of the children to teach them the words that they used every day. I found that really helped. Teaching like that I was able to bring the test scores of those kids up.

I also took a course in astronomy, studying the stars. The reason why I took that one was I said, "They're looking at the skies every day and every night, and it's good to be able to talk about it." The course showed me how to talk about this to the children, and they could learn those words from me.

I also felt that I needed to get some college work about working with people in rural areas, and for that I went to

Atlanta University, in Atlanta, Georgia. I was there in the summer of 1937, while W. E. B. DuBois was teaching there. Since he was one of the greatest black intellectuals in the country, I enrolled in his class, "Interpersonal Relationships of Human Beings."

One afternoon I got on a streetcar to go to his class. I sat in the back, where blacks had to sit. From there I watched a black woman enter, with a baby in her arms and what looked like a two-year-old by the hand. He sat down in the front seat and said, "I'm Momma's little man, and I can sit up here."

His mother was so nervous that she shook. "No, come on, come on back," she said as she led him from the front seat to the back of the bus.

That afternoon we had class with DuBois, and I was telling about it. He said, "Yes, we have to tell our children that they have to sit in the back. They're not any worse than anybody else, but the laws of the state are such that they have to sit in the back of the bus. But tell them that there will come a time when this will be changed."

Of course, DuBois had been through a lot himself. When his first-born child had died at the age of eighteen months, DuBois didn't want to bury him in Georgia. He didn't want the prejudiced soil of Georgia to cover the body of his first-born child. He and his wife took the child's body back to Massachusetts for burial.

Anyway, he said in class that there will come a time when this will be changed. Some of those black people in that class hadn't been too long from the plantation, and some of them were still living on contract farms, which are so much like plantations. They would be saying, "What she bring that up for? You know, she just wants to start something." They didn't think too well of me. They thought I was a terribly controversial person, just stirring up trouble by talking.

But nevertheless, I went on, and I got to the place where I had to give my concerns regardless of where I was. The problem, I realized, was not only whites against blacks. It was men against women; it was old against young. You had all those things to fight all the time regardless, and it's still a constant fight.

In those early years in Charleston I redoubled my efforts to earn enough credits to win my Bachelor of Arts degree. But it was not until 1942 that Benedict College in Columbia conferred on me that degree which I had been so long pursuing.

Having my bachelor's degree, I felt I should try for a master's. I enrolled at Hampton Institute at Hampton, Virginia, in the summer of 1944. For three summers I worked and was able to get my master's. When I left Columbia in 1947 after being there eighteen years, my salary had advanced from $780 a year to almost $4000 a year.

While I was teaching in Columbia, I worked on the problem of getting equal pay for teachers. Each school district set its own salaries, and usually the black teachers got about half of what the white teachers were paid.

One white teacher let us see her check. We compared it to that of one black teacher, who had the same amount of training and had been working the same time.

The New York office of the NAACP sent down one of its top lawyers, Thurgood Marshall. We presented the case to him, and he took it to court. The judge in that federal court was the man I've told you about from Charleston, Judge Waring. In 1945 he ruled that black and white teachers with equal qualifications had to get equal salaries. So that was a great triumph for us.

Then the school authorities decided that black teachers would have to take a test, the National Teacher Exam. There were forty-two of us who took it the first time, and for those of us who made "A" our salaries went from $62.50 a month to $117.00 a month. I thought I was wealthy then.

In Columbia I could mix with people that I couldn't in Charleston because my father was a former slave and my mother took in laundry. Columbia was more democratic. There I learned to feel comfortable with middle-class people, even though I never really considered myself a middle-class person.

While I was living in Columbia my mother had a stroke. It was very severe, and I used to come back and forth from Columbia every weekend to see about her. Her mouth was twisted, and her neck was in terrible condition. When I would come on the weekends, the woman who was taking care of her during the week would try to turn the neck. I knew it must have been very painful because sweat broke out over her forehead, and she was in terrible pain for a while. But we did it day after day until we got that mouth back in place and the neck so she could turn it.

After coming back and forth for practically a year, I decided that I would try to teach in Charleston. I came home and started living with her. And you know, she got real well again, so much so that she could cut wood at the age of ninety.

I felt that I couldn't stay in Columbia. Coming down from Columbia at that time on the bus was hard. Segregation was at its height. I would get on a bus in the afternoon, and no matter how long the trip you never could use a bathroom. We stopped at certain places where there were restrooms, but black people couldn't use them. We had to go up in the bushes.

One day when I was coming down to Charleston, there was another black woman. She must have been taking some medicine of some kind, and she ran into the restroom that was marked for whites. Back on the bus a white woman said to her: "You didn't see that sign, did you?"

The black woman replied, "I wasn't looking for the sign. I was looking for the same thing you were looking for, and that was that hole."

I said to myself, "Now, we've got to do something about these things," and that's what I did for the next twenty-four years.

Retirement and Contentment

WHILE I WAS WORKING with the Southern Christian Leadership Conference, my sister was living in the house on Henrietta Street that I had bought in 1927. It was on that same one-block street where we had grown up. I loved that old house—it had six large rooms of varying sizes. Three were strung out in box-car fashion, with three more on top of them. Each room opened onto the piazza, the long narrow porch that ran along one side of the house.

But the neighborhood had become unsafe. It got to the place where the boys down the street wouldn't let our mail stay in our mail box because my sister was at school teaching all day and I was away. When the mailman would come with checks, the boys would take them out.

One night I was in Minnesota. The American Friends Service Committee had sent me to a little town right out from Minneapolis, Minnesota, and while there I called my sister. She said she didn't want to talk because boys were taking hubcaps off the automobiles of the people who were in church. She was afraid that if she would call the police, the boys would come and do some harm to her. When I came home from there, I noticed that she was taking the carving knives upstairs with her at night. She was afraid someone would break into that kitchen (it was right on the yard) and would take the knives and do her some harm

I felt that rather than to live with fear like that, it is better to try to move. I wanted a home in a neighborhood I thought would be a little bit more safe, because I was still traveling, and my granddaughter was here going to school. I looked about two years before I found this house about two miles north of Henrietta Street in a middle-class neighborhood. We moved in here two days before Christmas, 1966. I was coming from Camden, Alabama, and everything was so clean we could just have our Christmas dinner and enjoy ourselves.

I was sixty-eight years old, and a whole lot of people said to me that buying a house was too big an undertaking at my age. But I tried it anyhow. I sank all my money in this house. It was aged, so I had to have lots of work done on it. Some people will go under with repairs like I've had, but I really trust in God and feel that I'm coming out. I just knock on lead at times. Money never did worry me much. I never had much, so I just made whatever I had do.

In the summer of 1970 I officially retired from SCLC. So much had been accomplished that I felt all right about giving up my travels. Then, too, my sister had Parkinson's disease and needed me to be at home to care for her.

SCLC held a banquet for me at the Francis Marion Hotel, right down on that Union Square where I hauled water from the fountain as a girl. At the banquet, I told everyone that "The air has finally gotten to the place that we can breathe it together." They presented me the Martin Luther King, Jr., Award with this inscription: "To Septima Poinsette Clark for Great Service to Humanity."

For many years, because of my outspoken ways, I was tabooed by both whites and blacks. But lately I have beeen getting a lot of recognition. It actually started in 1960 when I got a plaque from the Utilities Club of New York. Since that time I have gotten many plaques. The National Education Association gave me its Race Relations Award in 1976, and I went to Washington in 1979 to receive a Living Legacy Award from President Carter.

Here in Charleston my name is known because a day care center is named for me, and part of the new expressway through town is called the Septima P. Clark Expressway. The women of two black churches in Charleston have come forth with certificates of appreciation for the work I have done. One is a small Methodist church and the other a small

Baptist church. Now it has come to the place that they see that the work I was doing was really worthwhile. I'm very glad that I had enough patience and enough of the non-violent philosophy within me that I could take it and not be bitter towards any of them. They were afraid, but I wasn't.

Some people here are still afraid. The big churches with the middle-class members are still a little bit afraid to say anything. I belong to a sorority called Alpha Kappa Alpha, and quite a number of my sorority members are still afraid of me and still worry about the articles that come out in the paper saying that I helped to get black teachers in Charleston or I helped to get equalization of salaries for black teachers. They are still concerned about that, although they are profiting by it. But they still feel concerned. They get afraid of things. Peace and contentment, that's what you need.

Education is my big priority right now. I want people to see children as human beings and not to think of the money that it costs nor to think of the amount of time that it will take, but to think of the lives that can be developed into Americans who will redeem the soul of America and will really make America a great country. This is my feeling now.

I am serving my second term on the school board of Charleston County. The local teachers' union paid my fee to run the first time in 1976, because they knew that I would speak out in their behalf. One black man had served before me, but no black woman ever had. I celebrated my 78th birthday by winning in 1976.

Right now we have a school board made up of a number of businessmen. They are not very much concerned about the teachers, so I'm still in the minority.

But since I'm the first black woman who ever was on that board, I have to play it evenly. In the paper the other day, when they were talking about the board's not giving teachers bonuses, they said, "Mrs. Clark had a list of fifty-six teacher vacancies, and she's wondering how you are going to get teachers to come into this county." I wanted them to think about that. If you don't offer the teachers something, what are you going to have?

Septima Clark on the porch of her home on President Street in Charleston, 1979.

LARRY CAMERON

We do have problems. But I have lived so long that I have seen great progress. A lot of people think that it's terrible, and they are worried about the things that are happening today. I'm not, because out of the chaos, I feel, has come great thinking.

I've been talking about simple justice for quite some time. Of course, I've lived through so much that I do not expect to see justice until about a hundred years from now because attitudes are so slow to change.

Another thing I am working on is fighting for my pension and back pay. When I was teaching in Charleston, my retirement funds were put into a state pension, and that was all taken away when I was fired. In 1976 the National Educational Association started airing my case all over the United States, and then the state legislature decided to pay me a pension of $3600 each year.

But numbers of lawyers have told me that the state still owes me that pay from 1956 to 1964, when I would have been teaching if I had not been unjustly fired. It amounts to $36,412. They want me to press charges against the state for that amount, but I say no. I'm going to do it non-violently. I've sent letters to all the representatives and to some of the senators and to the NAACP man, and they are all for me to get my back pay. They told me that this year it did not reach the budget. It might get there next year; I'll be waiting for it when it comes.★

If I were young again, starting all over, I'd do the same things over and over again. I feel that. I don't think my ideas would change. My philosophy is such that I'm not going to vote against the oppressed. I have been oppressed, and so I am always going to have a vote for the oppressed, regardless of whether that oppressed is black or white or yellow or the people of the Middle East, or what. I have that feeling.

But I really do feel that this is the best part of life. It's not that you have just grown old, but it is how you have grown old. I feel that I have grown old with dreams that I want to come true, and that I have grown old believing there

★ In July, 1981, the state legislature approved paying Mrs. Clark her back pay.

is always a beautiful lining to that cloud that overshadows things. I have great belief in the fact that whenever there is chaos, it creates wonderful thinking. I consider chaos a gift, and this has come during my old age.

When I die, I don't want to have elaborate things. I would rather my money be spent to put milk in the stomachs of babies rather than on a plush metallic casket to put down in the ground. I don't see the use of having silk and satin put on your body, when all of that money can be left for children. I really don't want to have all this plush stuff that people are talking about today. The undertakers are making so much money. You can buy a box for $60 or so, and they will charge you over $2000. I just think that that is a waste of money.

Poor people in the country used to think that was some thing they had to do—dress up the dead and have this great big funeral. They didn't when I first went over there. They used to make their own coffins. The man whose house I lived in, the Reverend Jenkins, made the coffins and lined them with a piece of sheet. It's just as good because, after all, when you're dead, you're dead.

Let me be modest and simple. This is the way I think I should be. This is the way I think I should die. This is the way I think I should be buried, with the goodwill of the people knowing that I was willing to give service. I said to the man that I spoke for on Sunday, when he said, "Mrs. Clark, what are you going to charge?" I said, "If you want to give me something, give me. But don't ask me to charge you, not for service."

If I would sum up my life, I think of a little mischievous girl who would speak back to her mother, and her mother would flog her for doing just that. I would think of the young woman who dared to speak out in groups about the things that she thought were not right, whether it was at home or church or school or the community—wherever I was. If I had to think of myself when I became a middle-aged woman, I think of the many dangers that I had to go into, working in the eleven deep south states and five fringe states, and still these things did not make me feel afraid nor ashamed. And now in my old age I'm still working, helping young people to get financial aid for college, lecturing to them to see that they try to put on the non-violent attitude, and also working as a member of the school board to see that teachers become dedicated persons, not only in this county, but all over as they work in national organizations.

Don't ever think that everything went right. It didn't. Many times there were failures. But we had to mull over those failures and work until we could get them ironed out. The only reason why I thought the Citizenship School Program was right was because when people went down to register and vote, they were able to register and vote. They received their registration certificate. Then I knew that what I did must have been right. But I didn't know it before. It was an experiment that I was trying. When I went into communities and talked to people, I couldn't say that I was saying the right thing. But as I saw people work in these communities, and decide to attempt some of the things that were recommended, then succeed in doing things like being able to get checks signed at banks and getting recognized in the community among their own people and in their churches, then I knew that that experiment had worked out. But I couldn't be sure that the experiment was going to work. I don't think anybody can be sure. You just try and see if it's coming.

As we go along, it's going to take that hundred years for attitudes to change. They will change. There will be warm spots in the hearts of many whites, who will see what we need to do for people—low-income people, whites and blacks, Cubans, and all others. We've got to learn to work with all of them. I don't expect to ever see a utopia. No, I think there will always be something that you're going to have to work on, always. That's why, when we have chaos and people say, "I'm scared. I'm scared. I'm concerned," I say, "Out of that will come something good." It will, too. They can be afraid if they want to, afraid of what is going to happen. Things will happen, and things will change. The only thing that's really worthwhile is change. It's coming.

CHRONOLOGY

May 3, 1898	Septima Poinsette born in Charleston, South Carolina
September 1916	Septima Poinsette began teaching on Johns Island
May 23, 1920	Septima Poinsette married Nerie Clark
1929–1947	Septima Clark in Columbia, South Carolina
June 1947	Septima Clark returned to Charleston
1948	South Carolina primaries opened to black voters
May 17, 1954	Supreme Court ruled segregation in schools unconstitutional
December 1, 1955	Rosa Parks refused to give up seat in Montgomery bus
May–June 1956	Septima fired in Charleston, hired by Highlander Folk School
November 13, 1956	Supreme Court ruled segregation on buses unconstitutional
January 1957	First Citizenship School on Johns Island
March 1957	Founding of Southern Christian Leadership Conference (SCLC)

July 31, 1959	Raid on Highlander Folk School
February 1, 1960	First sit-in, Greensboro, North Carolina
April 15, 1960	Student Non-violent Coordinating Committee (SNCC) founded
May 1961	Freedom rides
Summer 1961	Citizenship School Program transferred to SCLC
December 1961	Highlander closed by state; re-opened in Knoxville
April–May 1963	Birmingham demonstrations
August 28, 1963	March on Washington
November 22, 1963	President John F. Kennedy killed
Summer 1964	Freedom Summer
December 10, 1964	Rev. M. L. King, Jr., received Nobel Peace Prize
March 21–25, 1965	March from Selma to Montgomery, Alabama
August 6, 1965	President Johnson signed the Voting Rights Act
April 4, 1968	Rev. M. L. King, Jr., killed
June 19, 1970	Septima Clark retired from SCLC

NOTES ON SOURCES

The story told by E.D. Nixon at the beginning of "Finding Rosa Parks" is from Howell Raines, ed., *My Soul Is Rested: Movement Days in the Deep South Remembered* (New York: Bantam, 1978), pp. 43–44.

Septima Clark told me the bulk of her story in my interviews with her in Charleston from August 27–September 2, 1979, and again on July 3–6, 1984. I checked her story for consistency by comparing her account to me with her accounts to other interviewers: interviews with Eliot Wigginton, June 20, 1981, Highlander Center Archives; with Peter Wood, February 3, 1981, Highlander Center Archives; with Eugene Walker, July 30, 1976, and with Jacquelyne Hall, July 25, 1981, both in the Southern Oral History Program Collection, Southern Historical Collection, University of North Carolina-Chapel Hill. I also used for comparison Septima Clark's published autobiography: *Echo in My Soul* (New York: E.P. Dutton & Co., 1962).

I interviewed other people who helped me put the story together. Chiefly those talks were the following:

Interviews with Myles Horton, October 25–November 5, 1981, October, 1983, June, 1984; with Virginia Durr, December 7, 1980; with Bernice Robinson, July 5, 1984.

Transcript of Rosa Parks' speech at a testimonial dinner held in Berkeley, May 1, 1980.

Other primary sources that I consulted to fill in the context were:

Blake, J. Herman. "Citizen Participation, Democracy and Social Change." A Report to the Emil Schwartzhaupt Foundation, Dec. 1, 1969.

Cotton, Dorothy. Interviewed by Eliot Wigginton, Highlander Center Archives.

Papers of the Southern Christian Leadership Conference, 1954–1970, in the Archives of the Martin Luther King, Jr., Center for Social Change, Atlanta, GA.

"Rosa Parks Reporting on the Bus Boycott." Recorded at Highlander, March 3–4, 1956. Highlander Center Archives.

"Rosa Parks, Myles Horton, and E.D. Nixon in Conversation with Studs Terkel in Chicago, on Radio, June 8, 1973." Transcript, Highlander Center Archives.

Young, Andrew. Interviewed by Eliot Wigginton, July 8, 1981. Highlander Center Archives.

Waring, J. Waties, Oral History, Columbia University Collection. Interviews made from January 1956–March 1957.

Many of the standard works about the civil rights movement overlook the significance of women like Rosa Parks and Septima Clark. The following published sources proved to be the most helpful in assembling this story:

Burt, Olive. *Black Women of Valor.* New York: Julian Messner, 1974.

Carawan, Guy and Candie. *Ain't You Got a Right to the Tree of Life?* New York: Simon and Schuster, 1966. A beautiful book about Johns Island, with photographs, songs, and interviews.

Clark, Septima. "Literacy and Liberation." *Freedomways* (First Quarter, 1964), 113–124.

Derkes, Scott. "Dat Not Be My Echo." *South Carolina Wildlife* 26, 4 (July/August 1979), 44–49. Features Septima Clark, about the language on the off-shore islands.

Drago, Edmund L. and Eugene Hunt. *A History of Avery Normal Institute from 1865–1954.* Pamphlet, no date.

Edgerton, John. "The Trial of Highlander." *Southern Exposure* VI, 1 (n.d.), 82–89.

Fields, Mamie with Karen Fields. *Lemon Swamp and Other Places: A Carolina Memoir.* New York, The Free Press, 1983. A memoir of Charleston by a middle-class black woman, ten years older than Septima Clark, who also taught on Johns Island, good for the nuances of color and class.

Gallman, Vanessa. "Septima Clark: On Life, Courage, Dedication." *View South* I, 4 (July/August, 1979), 13–16.

Giddings, Paula. *When and Where I Enter: The Impact of Black Women on Race and Sex in America.* New York: William Morrow, 1984. Chapter XV, "Dress Rehearsal for the Sixties," is especially helpful on the role of women in the Fifties.

Grafton, Samuel. "The Lonesomest Man in Town." *Collier's* (April 29, 1950), pp. 20–21. A fine feature about Judge Waring.

Lawson, Steven F. *Black Ballots: Voting Rights in the South, 1944–1969.* New York: Columbia University Press, 1976.

Lewis, David L. *King: A Biography.* 2nd ed. Urbana: University of Illinois Press, 1978. Chapter 3 is the best description of what happened in Montgomery that I found.

Morris, Aldon D. *The Origins of the Civil Rights Movement: Black Communities Organizing for Change.* New York: The Free Press, 1984.

Raines, Howell, ed. *My Soul Is Rested: Movement Days in the Deep South Remembered.* New York: Bantam, 1978.

Richardson, Joe M. "Francis L. Cardozo: Black Educator During Reconstruction." *Journal of Negro Education* (Winter 1979), pp. 73–83.

Tjerandsen, Carl. *Education for Citizenship: A Foundation's Experience*. Santa Cruz, CA: Emil Schwarzhaupt Foundation, 1980.

Waring, Laura Witte. *The Way It Was In Charleston*. Thomas R. Waring, Jr., ed. Old Greenwich, Conn.: Devin-Adair Co., 1980.

Woodward, C. Van. *The Strange Career of Jim Crow*. 3rd rev. ed. New York: Oxford University Press, 1974.

Voter Education Project Report. "A History of VEP and Race and Class in Southern Politics." Atlanta: VEP, no date.